NO PIGS ALLOWED

A Biblical Guide To Spiritual Warfare, Deliverance and Freedom

David Lawe
New York, New York

Unless otherwise stated, scriptures are quoted from the King James Version.

Publishing, Editing, format & Layout: Go'Judah Publishing House

ISBN 13: **978-0-9981777-7-9** ISBN 10: **0-9981777-7-9** **(paperback)**
ISBN 13: **979-8-950439-00-1** ISBN 10: **8-950439-00-1** **(e-pub)**

www.gojudah.com 1-855-GO'JUDAH X 205

DEDICATION

This book is dedicated to the phenomenal woman I am honored to call my wife, the one who has walked beside me through every season of life and consistently reminded me of the champion within. Your strength, grace, and unwavering support have shaped my journey in ways words cannot fully express. You are truly one of a kind. I am eternally grateful. Love you!

PREFACE

This book was birthed out of more than two decades of study, prayer, and lived experience. It did not emerge from a comfortable office with clean theological frameworks. It was forged in the middle of real ministry, sitting across from real people who carried real pain, navigating the kind of bondage that does not respond to advice alone and does not yield to a single prayer. Over the years, I have encountered many individuals struggling with demonic oppression in specific areas of their lives, issues that produced persistent, seemingly untreatable negative behavior patterns. What I observed in those encounters, and what I have wrestled through personally, is what you now hold in your hands.

I have observed that these patterns are often accompanied by what I refer to as P.I.G.S. Pain, Iniquity, Guilt, and Strongholds. Pain may appear in physical, emotional, social, or mental forms, and it is rarely as simple as it looks. Iniquity represents willful, habitual, or premeditated wrongdoing that dulls and eventually destroys one's moral compass through repetition. Guilt is the internal weight and torment that follows after actions or experiences that violate one's values. It is like a prison built without bars. Strongholds are the entrenched mindsets, beliefs, or behaviors that keep individuals stuck, limited, and oppressed long after the original wound should have healed. This book is not a theory on paper. It is a revelation that has been tested through trials, victories, failures, and the unwavering grace of God. There have been seasons in my own life when I confronted the "pigs" I am writing about. There have been moments when I sat in the discomfort of my own unresolved areas and had to choose between comfort and transformation. Every word in this book carries the weight of that journey. This book is designed to hand you both the spiritual strategies and practical principles to ensure that freedom becomes your reality.

The title itself needs no elaborate explanation. "Pigs" in the biblical and cultural imagination represent the unclean, the unwanted, the inappropriate, and the unrighteous. They manifest as destructive habits, toxic relationships, unhealthy cycles, negative mindsets, persistent strongholds, and spiritual blockages. They often disguise themselves as harmless or familiar, and that familiarity is precisely what makes them dangerous. Over time, what was once foreign begins to feel like home. What was once conviction begins to feel like condemnation. What was once a battle begins to feel like an identity.

My prayer is this: as you journey through these pages, you will receive more than information. May you receive transformation. May every chapter function as a key to a door you have been standing outside of for far too long. The Word of God declares,

"Whom the Son sets free is free indeed." **John 8:36**

That freedom is not hypothetical. It is not reserved for the spiritually elite or the theologically trained. It belongs to anyone who is willing to pursue it with the same desperation they once reserved for their bondage. I wrote this book for you. Whoever you are. Wherever you are. Whatever is living in your life that does not belong there, it is time for it to leave. I also want you to know something important before you turn the first page: the fact that you are holding this book is not an accident. People do not stumble accidentally into the kind of material that confronts bondage and demands honesty. You were drawn here. Something in you recognized that it was time. Time to stop managing what should be evicted, time to stop normalizing what was never supposed to be normal, time to finally address the things that have been quietly limiting your life for longer than you care to remember. That recognition is the voice of God. That drawing is the beginning of the work He intends to complete in you through these pages.

As you encounter each chapter, I encourage you to adopt the **"No Pigs Allowed"** declaration not merely as a motivational phrase but as a spiritual boundary you enforce daily. Speak it in the morning. Declare it when temptation knocks. Say it when old habits whisper your name. Every time you proclaim it, you are drawing a line in the soil of your soul and saying to everything unclean: you do not have permission to live here.

TABLE OF CONTENTS

SECTION I........EXPOSURE: Reclaiming Your Territory..10

Chapter 1: The Intruder: Guarding Your Territory..11

Chapter 2: The Ugly Truth: Confronting What You Have Tolerated....................................23

SECTION II........EXCAVATION: Breaking Open the Wounds.....................................34

Chapter 3: Are You Covered?: The Necessity of Spiritual Alignment...................................35

Chapter 4: Five Smooth Stones: Preparation Before Confrontation.....................................45

Chapter 5: The Struggle: Understanding the War Within...57

SECTION III........SABOTEURS: Recognizing the Enemies Within..............................68

Chapter 6: The Spirit of Absalom: When Pride Seeks the Throne..69

Chapter 7: The Garage Door: When Access Is Quietly Granted..79

SECTION IV...INTERNAL BONDAGES: Untying the Soul and Restoring Alignment......88

Chapter 8: Soul Ties: When Attachment Becomes Entanglement..89

Chapter 9: Wholeness: When Alignment Becomes Integration..97

SECTION V...VIGILANCE: Managing Post-Deliverance Vulnerability 110

Chapter 10: The Danger Zone: Guarding What Has Been Restored...................................111

Chapter 11: Jewels from the Pigpen: Wisdom Extracted from Consequence.......................121

SECTION VI....GOVERNANCE: Living as a Champion and Sustaining Victory............135

Chapter 12: The Champion: Formed for Dominion...136

Chapter 13: Sustained Change: Building What Endures..149

Conclusion 159

Glossary 163

Bibliography 169

Index 171

P — Pain I — Iniquity G — Guilt S — Strongholds

"For we wrestle not against flesh and blood, but against principalities, against powers, against the rulers of the darkness of this world, against spiritual wickedness in high places."

Ephesians 6:12

SECTION I

EXPOSURE

Reclaiming Your Territory

— — —

Before the unwanted can be removed, it must first be revealed. There are intrusions in life that do not announce themselves loudly. They settle quietly. They normalize gradually. They blend into the rhythm of daily routine until what was once foreign becomes familiar, and what was once alarming begins to feel like simply the way things are. You stop noticing the weight because you have carried it for so long. You stop questioning the pattern because it has become part of your story. And slowly, almost imperceptibly, the intruder becomes a resident.

This section confronts the uncomfortable beginning of freedom: exposure. Exposure is not condemnation. It is mercy. It is the moment when light enters places that darkness has convinced you were permanent. It is the turning point where you stop coexisting with what does not belong and start confronting it with the authority that God has already placed in your hands. You cannot guard territory you refuse to examine. You cannot evict what you will not name. You cannot confront what you have quietly tolerated. In these opening chapters, you will face intrusion, self-deception, and the tolerated compromises that have been quietly draining your life. Not to shame you but to restore governance. Territory must be reclaimed before it can be protected.

CHAPTER ONE
THE INTRUDER

Guarding Your Territory

"The thief cometh not, but for to steal, and to kill, and to destroy: I am come that they might have life, and that they might have it more abundantly."

John 10:10

There are things in your life that do not belong there. Not everything that grows in your house was planted by God. Not every thought that repeats itself deserves residence. Not every habit that feels familiar is covenant-aligned. Before freedom becomes possible, intrusion must be acknowledged because you cannot evict what you refuse to identify.

I want to begin with a picture that most of us have never thought about carefully enough. When a professional thief selects a target, it is never random. The image of a burglar acting on impulse, pulling up to a house on a whim, and breaking in is almost entirely a fiction. In reality, theft is the end result of a process that began long before the break-in occurred. A skilled thief studies the house. He drives past it multiple times. He learns the patterns of the people who live there, what time the lights come on, when the cars leave in the morning, and how long the driveway stays empty in the afternoon. He maps the rhythms of the household over days, sometimes weeks. He looks for the weakest point: the unlocked window, the unlit side entrance, the door that does not close completely. And only when he is confident that access is available and resistance is minimal does he move.

What this tells us is profoundly important. Intrusion is always preceded by observation. The enemy of your soul operates by the same principle. He does not force his way in recklessly. He studies your patterns. He identifies your vulnerabilities. He watches what you neglect, what you avoid dealing with, what emotional doors you leave propped open. He is patient. And when access becomes available through hurt, disappointment, unresolved sin, or simple neglect, he enters. Not with a dramatic announcement, but quietly. And once inside, he begins to settle. As I write this chapter, I am reminded of the scriptural premise of this book. In Matthew chapter 8, Jesus and his disciples arrived in Gadarenes. They were immediately met by two men. Their profile was chilling: possessed with demons, dwelling among the dead, violently territorial, and so fierce that no one dared pass that way. When they saw Jesus, the demonic presence within them instantly recognized Him: "What do you want with us, Son of God?" they shouted. "Have you come here to torment us before the appointed time?" (Matthew 8:29). Nearby, a large herd of pigs was feeding. The demons begged Jesus, "If you drive us out, send us into the herd of pigs. "Notice Jesus didn't choose the pigs for them. They requested it. Why? Because evil spirits crave a physical host to continue their destructive assignments. Jesus simply said, "Go!" And in that moment, the men were freed. The spirits then entered the pigs, who immediately stampeded down a steep bank into the water and drowned. Pigs are naturally capable of swimming and, in fact, are known to be strong swimmers. Their ability to swim shows that, by design, they were equipped with the strength and instinct to survive in various environments. However, in Matthew chapter 8, the herd of pigs that became possessed by demons ended up drowning in the sea. This wasn't because they lacked the physical ability to swim, but because the demonic spirits fulfilled their assignment. Here's the key to this bible story: This moment wasn't just about two tormented men. This was about the disruption of unrighteous practices, and Jesus seized the opportunity to evict the unseen intruders.

The Anatomy of Intrusion

Scripture makes this plain. The thief, Jesus says, comes not to visit but to occupy, to steal, to kill, to destroy. These are not three separate activities. They describe a single progressive reality. What is stolen first is peace. Then identity is attacked. Then purpose comes under assault. The thief does not do all of this at once because that would alert you. He is strategic. He begins with small thefts, minor compromises, subtle distortions, familiar temptations and gradually escalates as habitation deepens.

Many believers are fighting symptoms when they should be confronting intrusion. The anxiety that will not lift, the recurring pattern of sin that shame alone cannot break, the emotional instability that seems disproportionate to circumstance, the anger that boils within for an injustice that was served to you, the pride and resentment that keep resurfacing despite genuine repentance, these are often not random occurrences. They are evidence of territory left unguarded. They are symptoms pointing to an access point that was never properly sealed.

This is why exposure is so essential. Exposure is the moment you stop treating the symptom and start examining the source. It is the willingness to ask not just "What is happening to me?" but "How did this get in? When did I stop guarding this? What did I allow that I should have refused?" These questions are not comfortable. But they are the questions that lead to lasting freedom rather than temporary relief.

The Three-Stage Strategy of the Thief

John 10:10 gives us three verbs that describe the thief's complete agenda: steal, kill, and destroy. These are not three random activities; they represent a deliberate progression. Theft comes first because the enemy understands that what is taken quietly is rarely recovered. When something is stolen gradually, through incremental compromise and normalized dysfunction, the person who loses it often does not notice the loss until the damage has accumulated beyond what feels easily reversible. Peace is stolen first; the quiet confidence of a person who knows who they are and where they stand. Without peace, the interior life becomes noisy and disoriented.

From peace, the assault moves to identity. Once you are disoriented, once the ground beneath your spiritual confidence has been destabilized, the voice of the intruder begins to redefine you. "This is just who you are." "You have always been this way." "You will never overcome this." These are not random thoughts, they are targeted identity statements designed to replace the truth of who God says you are with a smaller, more manageable narrative that keeps you contained. Identity theft is arguably the most devastating form of spiritual robbery because it shapes every subsequent decision. When you do not know who you are, you cannot govern your territory. You cannot resist what you have come to believe is simply part of you.

The third stage, “destruction,” is what happens when theft and identity assault go unaddressed long enough that the accumulated damage reshapes the entire trajectory of a life. Purpose is lost.

Relationships are fractured. The person who was designed for dominion finds themselves managing dysfunction instead of building legacy. This is the full agenda of the thief, and it is executed not through one dramatic attack but through patient, incremental occupation. Understanding the progression is the first line of defense against it. You cannot confront what you cannot name.

Dominion Was Part of the Original Design

The concept of territory is not peripheral to Scripture it is central to it. From the very beginning of the biblical narrative, God spoke a mandate of dominion into the identity of humanity.

> *"And God said, Let us make man in our image, after our likeness: and let them have dominion over the fish of the sea, and over the fowl of the air, and over the cattle, and over all the earth..."* **Genesis 1:26**

Dominion implies governance. Governance implies boundaries. Boundaries imply responsibility. If dominion was part of the original design, then guarding territory is not optional; it is the fulfilment of what God placed in us from the beginning. When you tolerate what contradicts your calling, you are not just making a personal mistake.

You are abdicating a divine responsibility. You are allowing the territory that God entrusted to your stewardship to be occupied by something that has no right to be there.

The intruder thrives where structure is absent. Neglected prayer creates access. Neglected accountability creates vulnerability. Neglected emotional honesty creates hiding places for what should be confronted. Neglect is not dramatic rebellion; it is the quiet form of abdication that most people never notice until the damage is already done.

> *"Submit yourselves therefore to God. Resist the devil, and he will flee from you."* **James 4:7**

Notice the order in that verse. Submission precedes resistance. You cannot resist effectively if you have not first aligned yourself under God's authority. Resistance without submission is not spiritual warfare, it is spiritual presumption. It is attempting to exercise an authority you have not properly positioned yourself under. This is why many people pray fervently against their problems and see little change: they are trying to resist the enemy from a position of misalignment. Alignment with God is the prerequisite to effective resistance against the enemy.

Guarding Your Territory

The first step in sustained freedom is exposure. Not emotional release, not dramatic spiritual experience, not simply attending more services or reading more devotionals. Exposure. You must name the intruder. You must trace the access point. You must refuse the return narrative, the voice that tells you this is just how you are; this is your struggle, this is your story. And you must build structure after eviction, because an empty house is not a free house. It is simply a vacant one, and vacant spaces invite reoccupation.

What God is asking you to do in this chapter is not complicated, but it will require courage. He is asking you to look honestly at your life, your thought patterns, your emotional cycles, your behavioral habits, your relational tendencies, and to ask with full sincerity: What is living here that does not belong? What has been here so long that I stopped questioning it? What have I normalized that God never ordained?

> *"Casting down imaginations, and every high thing that exalteth itself against the knowledge of God, and bringing into captivity every thought to the obedience of Christ."* **2 Corinthians 10:5**

Imagination must be governed. Thoughts must be examined. Agreements must be evaluated. If a thought, habit, relationship, or pattern exalts itself against the truth of who God says you are, it does not belong in your house. You are not a victim of your circumstances. You are a steward of your territory and stewardship begins with exposure.

REFLECTION

- What patterns have I normalized that contradict my calling?
- Where have I allowed neglect to create access in my life?
- What thought patterns need to be examined and cast down?
- Am I governing my territory or merely reacting to problems?

APPLICATION

- Identify one area of tolerated compromise and name it honestly.
- Establish one structural discipline this week to begin closing that access.
- Invite accountability in an area you have previously kept hidden.
- Pray specifically against the intrusion you have named, not generally for peace.

PRAYER

Father, expose what does not belong in my life. Give me clarity without condemnation and conviction without shame. Strengthen me to guard what You have entrusted to me. Teach me to govern my thoughts, my habits, and my environment with the authority You have placed within me. I choose stewardship. In Jesus' name, Amen.

DECLARATION:

I guard my territory.

I submit to God and resist the enemy.

I build structure where neglect once lived.

No pigs allowed!

CHAPTER TWO
THE UGLY TRUTH

Confronting What You Have Tolerated

"And ye shall know the truth, and the truth shall make you free."
John 8:32

Exposure reveals intrusion. Truth confronts tolerance. There is a particular kind of spiritual discomfort that comes not from discovering something new, but from acknowledging something you have known for a long time and chosen not to fully face. That is the ugly truth.

One of the most profound statements that has resonated with me throughout the years is derived from William Shakespeare, who writes with striking clarity, “To thine own self be true.” This statement, made by such a brilliant mind, should be embraced by all who seek true deliverance, because it is not merely a moral exhortation but a spiritual call to honesty before God. Its timeless wisdom serves as a compass for integrity, reminding us that authenticity is a firm foundation upon which real transformation can begin.

When one becomes aligned with their inner truth, external validation gradually loses its grip, pretension fades into the background, and vulnerability creates room for genuine change. This calls us to live from a place of deep self-awareness, where we are willing to stand before the mirror of truth and acknowledge where we truly are without disguise or excuse. It requires that we confront the scars, the wounds, and the brokenness within our lives without turning away.

Yet even in this process, there is comfort in knowing that beyond the layers formed by pressure, pain, and past experiences, there still exists the purest version of who we are, the person God intentionally created. The reality, however, is that embracing this truth involves confronting what is uncomfortable. The "ugly truth" is not about condemnation, but about honestly identifying the areas of our lives that need healing and correction. It is the courage to face your flaws, to admit your mistakes, and to recognize the evidence of what should not be present but has been allowed to remain.

At the same time, the ugly truth also reveals something deeper, which is that transformation is not only about what entered your life uninvited, but also about what was permitted to stay.

Sometimes it is about what you quietly permitted to remain, the habit you minimized, the pattern you excused, the narrative you protected because confronting it felt more threatening than living with it. Truth in Scripture is never merely informational. The word "know" in John 8:32 carries the weight of experiential, intimate recognition, the kind of knowing that penetrates self-deception and dismantles the internal story you have carefully constructed to avoid accountability. Freedom does not come from hearing truth occasionally. It comes from aligning with truth fully, repeatedly, and without the safety net of familiar excuses. There are five pillars for aligning with God's truth: decision, declarations, denouncing, discipline, and diversions. The first pillar is **Decision**; the intentional choice to confront reality rather than ignore or escape it. Once the decision is made, **declarations** follow, where truth is spoken with authority and conviction over the situation. The third pillar is **denouncing,** which involves rejecting lies, negative influences, and anything that opposes truth. **Discipline** then sustains the process, requiring consistent actions and habits that align with the truth you have chosen. Finally, **diversions** help redirect the mind and spirit away from destructive patterns toward healthy, constructive paths that reinforce growth and freedom.

The Power of Agreement

Agreement is one of the most underestimated spiritual forces in the life of a believer. What you agree with shapes what you become. This is not a motivational claim; it is a theological one rooted in how human beings are designed to function. The mind does not neutrally observe thoughts passing through it. It forms patterns. It builds architecture. Repeated exposure to a thought, a narrative, or a belief system produces grooves in the thinking that eventually become the default channels through which all subsequent experience is filtered.

This is why Scripture speaks of the renewing of the mind as an active, ongoing necessity rather than a one-time adjustment. The default architecture of the fallen mind is not neutral. It has been shaped by years of exposure to thoughts, voices, experiences, and agreements that did not originate in the truth of God's Word. And those years of shaping do not simply reverse themselves because a person becomes a believer. They must be actively dismantled and rebuilt through the sustained, intentional process of renewing the mind, replacing old agreements with new ones that are anchored in what is actually true.

The ugly truth often involves an agreement that was formed not in adulthood but in early life, a conclusion drawn from a painful experience that was never revisited and revised in the light of maturity and Scripture. A child who experiences abandonment may form an agreement that they are not worth staying for. An adolescent who experiences repeated failure in a particular area may form an agreement that they are fundamentally incapable. A young adult wounded by authority may form an agreement that submission leads to harm. These agreements are conclusions that made sense in the moment they were formed. But they persist in adulthood as governors of behavior, shaping decisions, limiting possibilities, and reinforcing themselves through the selective interpretation of new experiences.

The theology of ownership requires that we examine these agreements honestly, name them for what they are, and submit them to the authority of Scripture. Not the partial submission of acknowledging intellectually that a different thing is true while continuing to live from the old agreement, but the full submission of genuinely renouncing the lie and choosing to live from the truth. This is what Paul means by taking every thought captive. Not every thought that enters the mind deserves residence. Some thoughts are trespassers, and they must be treated as such.

The Prison of Self-Deception

One of the most sophisticated prisons in the human experience is the one we build from our own narratives. Self-deception is not stupidity. It is often the product of intelligence applied in the wrong direction, the mind's ability to construct convincing arguments for why the current situation is acceptable, inevitable, or someone else's fault. We become attorneys for our own dysfunction, building watertight cases for why change is too difficult, why our history justifies our habits, or why the standard simply does not apply to us in this particular instance.

Tolerance disguises itself in several forms. The most common is the language of identity: "That is just how I am." "That is how I was raised." "That is my struggle." These phrases feel like honesty, but they often function as termination points, places where examination stops and acceptance begins. The problem is that struggle is not identity. The Apostle Paul addresses this directly.

> *"Knowing this, that our old man is crucified with him, that the body of sin might be destroyed, that henceforth we should not serve sin."* **Romans 6:6**

Crucified does not mean restrained. It does not mean managed. It means executed. If the old man has been crucified with Christ, then the old man does not get to dictate present behavior. The ugly truth is this: some patterns persist not because they are stronger than God's grace, but because we have not yet fully renounced our agreement with them. Agreement gives power. When you repeatedly consent to a thought, entertaining it, rehearsing it, building your identity around it, it forms a narrative. When that narrative becomes internalized, it begins to govern decisions. If you do not govern your internal narrative, your internal narrative will govern your future.

The Theology of Ownership

There is a crucial theological movement that must happen on the road to freedom, and it is the movement from blame to ownership. This is not a self-help concept dressed in spiritual language. It is a biblical imperative. Healing cannot occur in an atmosphere of sustained blame, not because the hurt was not real, not because the wound was not inflicted unjustly, but because blame maintains a posture of powerlessness that locks you out of the authority God has already given you.

Ownership does not mean you caused everything that happened to you. It means you take responsibility for how you respond to everything that happened to you. It means you stop waiting for external circumstances to change before you begin to change internally. It means you say, with full sincerity: "I permitted this to continue. I entertained this. I agreed with this. And I am now choosing differently."

> *"He that covereth his sins shall not prosper: but whoso confesseth and forsaketh them shall have mercy."*
>
> **Proverbs 28:13**

Notice what that verse demands: not just confession, but forsaking. Many believers have mastered the language of confession without the lifestyle of forsaking. They confess the same sin repeatedly, sincerely, genuinely, and then return to the environment, the relationship, the habit that feeds it. Confession without forsaking is incomplete. And forsaking without honest confession is denial masquerading as discipline. Truth demands both.

Conviction Is Not Condemnation

One of the enemy's most effective strategies is to conflate conviction with condemnation in the mind of the believer. If he can convince you that the discomfort of being exposed is the same as being condemned, he can make you run from the very thing that would free you. Conviction feels uncomfortable. It is supposed to. It is the spiritual immune response, the body of Christ recognizing something foreign and raising the alarm. But conviction is directional. It points forward. It says: this is what needs to change, and here is the grace available to change it. Condemnation, by contrast, is not directional. It is paralyzing. It rehearses the past without offering a path. It defines you by your failure rather than by your potential in Christ. Romans 8:1 does not abolish conviction; it abolishes condemnation for those who are in Christ Jesus. The conviction you feel when you sit with this chapter is not God's judgment against you. It is His mercy toward you. God confronts what He intends to cleanse.

The ugly truth is not designed to shame you into paralysis. It is designed to free you from the sophisticated self-deception that has been your cell. You cannot heal what you refuse to expose. But exposure, when received in the context of grace, is not the end of your story. It is the beginning of your freedom.

REFLECTION

- What excuses have I rehearsed that prevent real change?
- Where have I blamed others for patterns that I have permitted to remain?
- Is there an area where I have agreed with a lie about who I am?
- Am I willing to confront what truth reveals, even if it is uncomfortable?

APPLICATION

- Write down one narrative you have believed about yourself that contradicts Scripture.

- Replace it with a specific biblical truth and meditate on it every day this week.
- Confess specifically, not generally, name the thing, not just the feeling.
- Take one measurable step toward forsaking the behavior you have tolerated.

PRAYER

Father, search me and reveal what I have tolerated. Remove self-deception. Give me courage to own what is mine and release what is not. Let Your Word divide truth from narrative and illuminate the places I have been avoiding. I receive conviction as mercy. I choose alignment over comfort. In Jesus' name, Amen.

DECLARATION

I embrace truth without reservation.
I reject self-deception.
I own what I have tolerated.
I align my narrative with Scripture.
I refuse the return narrative.
No pigs allowed!

SECTION II
EXCAVATION

Breaking Open the Wounds

– – –

Exposure reveals what is present. Excavation reveals why it remained.

Beneath visible behaviors lie deeper agreements. Beneath patterns lie permissions. Beneath habits lie narratives that were formed long before you were aware of what was being written on the walls of your soul. This section moves beyond surface correction into internal examination, not because surface correction is unimportant, but because it is insufficient on its own. You can change behavior without changing belief. You can modify actions without transforming the internal architecture that produces them. And when that happens, the behavior always returns, because the root was never addressed.

Struggle is rarely random. Repetition is rarely accidental. What persists has roots, emotional, relational, spiritual, and sometimes generational, that must be unearthed before genuine healing can take hold. Excavation requires honesty. It demands humility. It asks difficult questions about covering, discipline, preparation, and identity. But excavation is not destruction. It is preparation. When the soil is turned and the old is removed, foundations can finally be laid properly.

CHAPTER THREE

ARE YOU COVERED?

The Necessity of Spiritual Alignment

"Submit yourselves therefore to God. Resist the devil, and he will flee from you."

James 4:7

Exposure reveals intrusion. Truth confronts tolerance. But excavation asks a more difficult question, one that cuts closer to the bone: Why was there access in the first place? Why did the intruder find an entry point? Why did the pattern persist for as long as it did? The answer, more often than we are comfortable admitting, involves the question of covering. Many battles are lost long before they become visible. They are lost in isolation. They are lost in the quiet, proud independence that tells you that you do not need input, oversight, or accountability. They are lost when alignment is dismissed as unnecessary, when the protection of godly covering is rejected in favor of self-governance, and when the counsel of trustworthy voices is replaced by the echo chamber of your own perspective. And by the time the damage surfaces, the access point has been open for a long time.

What Covering Actually Means

Covering is one of the most misunderstood principles in the life of a believer. It is frequently reduced to institutional hierarchy, the organizational chart of a church or ministry, and in doing so, its true function is lost. Biblically understood, covering is protection through alignment. It is relational accountability under godly authority. It is not about who holds what title. It is about who has permission to speak into your life and challenge the blind spots that your own perspective cannot see. Having the right person to cover you ensures that while you are in transition, your vulnerability is guarded, and your transformation is nurtured. This person or group of people should be those who sees you beyond your faults and failures. They are not there to condemn but to correct in love, and to help guide you toward wholeness. They understand your insecurities, proclivities, and imperfections, but choose to stand with you until freedom is fully manifested in your life.

The relationship between submission and resistance in James 4:7 is instructive. Most believers want the second half of that verse without the first. They want the devil to flee, but they resist the prerequisite of submission. Authority flows from alignment. When you step outside divine order, when you decide you are mature enough to operate without input, accountable to no one, answerable to nothing outside your own judgment, you step outside the protection that alignment provides. And the enemy, who observes these things patiently, recognizes exposure and acts accordingly.

The Danger of Unexamined Isolation

The first rebellion in Scripture was not characterized by loud defiance. It was characterized by independent reasoning, reasoning apart from divine command, untethered from relational accountability, persuaded by a voice that offered the appearance of wisdom while producing destruction.

> *"And when the woman saw that the tree was good for food, and that it was pleasant to the eyes, and a*

tree to be desired to make one wise, she took of the fruit thereof..." **Genesis 3:6**

She reasoned apart from command. She evaluated independently. And in that moment of ungoverned autonomy, she opened an access point that changed human history. This is not a distant theological abstraction. It is the pattern that plays out in living rooms and prayer closets and ministry offices every day. When you stop receiving correction, when you stop being accountable to anyone who can honestly challenge your direction, you become vulnerable to the same subtle deception that began in a garden. Isolation sounds like wisdom. "I've grown beyond the need for that kind of oversight." "God speaks to me directly, I don't need a middleman." "I know what I'm doing." These are not the statements of a spiritually mature believer. They are the early warning signs of someone who has begun to drift and does not yet know it. Because isolation breeds narrative control, and narrative control protects self-justification, and self-justification is the fertile ground where strongholds grow unchallenged.

What Happens When Covering Is Rejected

The consequences of rejecting covering are rarely immediate and dramatic. They unfold gradually, in the quiet accumulation of unaddressed drift, unchallenged blind spots, and normalized compromise. When a person removes themselves from genuine accountability, whether through pride, through the accumulated weariness of past wounds from authority figures, or simply through the misidentification of independence as maturity, they begin a process of slow spiritual erosion that can be difficult to detect from the inside.

The first consequence is the loss of perspective check. Every human being has blind spots, areas of their character, their theology, and their behavior that they cannot see clearly because of proximity. The person who is genuinely covered has access to someone whose perspective is not limited by the same proximity. They can see what you cannot. They can name what you have normalized. They can ask the question that interrupts the drift before it becomes a pattern and the pattern before it becomes a lifestyle. When that voice is absent, the drift continues unchecked, and the person slowly loses the ability to accurately assess their own spiritual condition.

The second consequence is the reinforcement of self-justification. Isolation does not just remove correction; it creates the conditions in which the internal defense attorney becomes the only voice in the room. Without the counterweight of honest input, the narratives we construct about our own behavior become increasingly convincing. We rehearse them without challenge, refine them without examination, and eventually mistake the sophistication of our self-justification for genuine spiritual understanding. This is a dangerous place to live, because from the inside it feels like clarity, but from the outside it looks like the early stages of serious drift.

The third consequence is increased vulnerability to deception. Spiritual deception almost always follows isolation. The enemy does not simply attack the person who is genuinely covered and corrected. He waits for the uncovered season, the period of ungoverned independence, because he knows that a person who has removed themselves from accountability has also removed themselves from one of the primary means through which God protects His people. Covering is not a luxury for the spiritually immature. It is a structural necessity for everyone who is serious about sustained freedom.

Spiritual Maturity Is Measured by Governability

This is a truth that cuts against the grain of much contemporary Christian culture, which often equates spiritual maturity with independence. We celebrate the believer who has "graduated" beyond accountability, who operates with full autonomy, who answers to no one. But Scripture consistently presents a different picture. Spiritual maturity is measured not by independence but by governability, by the willingness to remain under authority, to receive correction, to be transparent about weakness, to allow others access to the places where drift is most likely to begin.

> *"But strong meat belongeth to them that are of full age, even those who by reason of use have their senses exercised to discern both good and evil."*
>
> **Hebrews 5:14**

Discernment is trained by use, and use includes the use of accountability, the practice of submitting your perceptions to trusted voices, and the discipline of allowing correction to shape your direction. You cannot grow without feedback. You cannot strengthen what you refuse to examine. You cannot protect territory effectively if you refuse alignment.

Covering does not mean you surrender your conscience or blindly follow anyone who claims authority. It means you acknowledge that your perspective has limits, that your blind spots are real, and that God often uses people as instruments of protection and correction in your life. The right covering corrects in love, prays with purpose, and refuses to exploit your vulnerability. If you are honest with yourself, ask: Were you uncovered when the intrusion occurred? Were you isolated? Did you drift without challenge? Was there a voice available that you chose not to hear?

REFLECTION

- Who currently has permission to correct me, and do I genuinely receive that correction?
- Do I resist feedback defensively, or do I receive it as protection?
- Have I mistaken independence for spiritual maturity?
- Where might isolation quietly create vulnerability in my life?

APPLICATION

- Identify one trusted voice and initiate intentional, ongoing accountability this week.
- Invite honest evaluation in one area where you tend to self-justify.
- Establish a rhythm of regular transparency rather than waiting for crises to confess.
- Examine honestly whether pride has limited your willingness to remain aligned.

PRAYER

Father, guard me from the pride of isolation. Teach me to value alignment over autonomy and protection over independence. Surround me with voices that sharpen and protect. Give me the humility to receive correction and the wisdom to remain accountable. I choose governability. In Jesus' name, Amen.

DECLARATION

I am aligned.

I am accountable.

I reject isolation.

I embrace correction.

I guard my territory through covering.

No pigs allowed!

CHAPTER FOUR
FIVE SMOOTH STONES

Preparation Before Confrontation

"The LORD that delivered me out of the paw of the lion, and out of the paw of the bear, he will deliver me out of the hand of this Philistine."
1 Samuel 17:37

Excavation exposes vulnerability. Alignment restores positioning. But preparation determines outcome. Before we can discuss how to truly overcome the "pigs" in your life, we must clearly and quickly understand that overcoming anything requires two main components. The first is intentionality and secondly persistence. For you to embrace victory, you must become prepense about defeating every opponent. This means that you wake up every morning with a mindset to purposefully overcome the piggy areas of your life. This should be one of your main focuses and not just one of your minute options. I believe that many people fail at drowning the "pigs" in their lives because they lack the passion accompanied by intentionality. It almost must become a life-or-death situation. If I don't fix this area of my life, or evict the "pigs", I cannot live fulfilled. Accompanied by your deliberate actions and premeditated mindset should be the virtue of relentlessness. This simply implies that if it does not happen the first try, you keep going until a change occurs. Look at the imagery of chopping down a big tree. It is inevitable for the tree to fall; however, it will take time and reinforcement. But I guarantee that if you keep chopping, eventually what once stood strong, tall, and seemed unbreakable will come tumbling down.

Many of the "pigs" in your life are not necessarily all physical things. Some of them, if not majority are invisible and intangible. They are forces that dwell in the mind, heart, and spirit, working silently to wear you down. Pay close attention to the biblical story of David. There is a truth embedded in the story of David and Goliath that most retellings miss entirely, and it is the truth that transforms the story from an inspiring narrative about a brave young man into a theological statement about how victory is produced. David did not defeat Goliath in the valley. He defeated him in obscurity, long before the confrontation became public. The valley was only the culmination of a preparation that had been happening in places where no one was watching, in the fields with the sheep, in the silence of the hillside, in the encounters with the lion and the bear that no crowd witnessed and no audience recorded. What appeared to be a sudden, dramatic moment of victory was the public expression of a private formation that had been taking shape for years.

The Seasons Nobody Sees

Between the anointing and the coronation, David spent years in the wilderness, hunted by Saul, living in caves, leading a band of men described in Scripture as everyone who was in distress, in debt, and discontented. These were not the years of a rising star. These were the years of a fugitive. And yet Scripture does not present these years as a waste. It presents them as formation.

Every person who is pursuing freedom and walking toward the authority God has designed for them will pass through their own version of the wilderness years. These are the seasons of preparation that do not feel like preparation, the periods of obscurity, difficulty, and apparent delay that seem to contradict what God has spoken over your life. In those seasons, the temptation is to conclude that either the promise was wrong or the process is taking too long. But the wilderness is not a detour from God's plan. It is the very path by which God shapes the character required to carry what He intends to give.

The smooth stones that David selected were shaped by the stream, by the slow, sustained pressure of water moving over them over time. Friction shaped them. They were not smooth when they came out of the quarry. They became smooth through the sustained, repeated experience of being pressed against what was harder than them. This is the theology of the wilderness season: God is pressing you against difficulty not to destroy you but to shape you. He is forming something in the seasons that nobody sees that will be deployed in the moment that everyone witnesses. The most important spiritual disciplines you will ever develop are the ones you establish when no one is watching, when there is no audience, no recognition, and no immediate reward. The prayer life you build in obscurity. The integrity you maintain when a compromise is easy and undetected.

The faithfulness you practice in the small assignments before the large ones come. These are the smooth stones. These are the formations that will determine whether your victory becomes a moment or a legacy.

What Goliath Really Represents

Goliath is more than a historical giant. He represents the recurring voice of opposition that has challenged your identity every time you have attempted to move forward in God. Notice what he said:

> *"And the Philistine said, I defy the armies of Israel this day; give me a man, that we may fight together."*
>
> **1 Samuel 17:10**

Defiance attacks identity before it attacks the body. Goliath's strategy was not primarily physical. It was psychological. He was attempting to redefine the army of Israel as incapable, intimidated, and defeated, before a single sword was drawn. And it worked for forty days. An entire army stood paralyzed not because they lacked weapons or physical strength, but because they had allowed a voice to occupy their minds and redefine their reality.

The “pigs” in your life often operate the same way. They speak before they act. They define before they destroy. They establish a narrative in your thinking, "You will never overcome this," "You have always been this way," "This is simply too powerful for you", and they rely on that narrative to maintain their position without ever having to fight for it. If they can win in your mind, they never need to win anywhere else.

Refusing Borrowed Armor

Before David selected his stones, he did something remarkable and theologically significant. He rejected Saul's armor.

> *"And David said unto Saul, I cannot go with these; for I have not proved them. And David put them off him."* **1 Samuel 17:39**

Saul's armor was not defective. It was simply not David's. It had not been formed through David's experiences. It had not been tested in David's battles. It was borrowed strength, external equipment that had not grown from internal formation. And David, with a spiritual discernment remarkable for his age, recognized that you cannot sustain victory with methods you have not tested privately.

This has immediate application. Many believers attempt to fight their battles with borrowed spiritual equipment, the testimony of someone else's deliverance, the formula from a conference, the method that worked for a different person in a different season. There is wisdom in learning from others. But there is no substitute for the stone that was shaped by your own experience of God's faithfulness. You need your own testimony of the lion. You need your own encounter with the bear. Private obedience produces public authority. Formation must precede confrontation.

The Five Smooth Stones

David selected five stones, not one. He prepared for multiple attempts, understanding that some giants do not fall on the first swing. The five smooth stones represent the structured disciplines of a prepared believer, not dramatic measures, but consistent formations. They were selected intentionally, shaped by friction, gathered with purpose.

The first stone is spiritual discipline, the daily practice of prayer, Scripture, worship, and fasting that forms the interior architecture of a free life. Discipline is not punishment; it is the infrastructure of sustained victory. Without it, even genuine breakthroughs fade because there is no structure to hold what was gained.

The second stone is mental renewal, the deliberate, ongoing work of replacing former narratives with scriptural truth. The forehead was the point of impact for David's stone, and that is not incidental. The mind is where giants speak. Intimidation targets thought before it targets action. If you do not govern your mind, the giants in your life will govern it for you.

> *"Casting down imaginations, and every high thing that exalteth itself against the knowledge of God, and bringing into captivity every thought to the obedience of Christ."* **2 Corinthians 10:5**

The third stone is emotional governance, the trained ability to recognize emotional triggers, resist reactive patterns, and respond from a place of alignment rather than impulse. Emotional vulnerability is one of the enemy's primary entry points. When fatigue, loneliness, discouragement, or grief are present without governance, access becomes available.

The fourth stone is relational accountability, the intentional cultivation of relationships in which honesty is expected and drift is challenged. You cannot guard your territory in isolation. You were not designed to. Accountability is not weakness. It is the structural reinforcement of what you are building.

The fifth stone is environmental boundaries, the deliberate management of spaces, relationships, content, and environments that shape your formation on a daily basis. If you consistently inhabit spaces that weaken your resolve, reinforce former patterns, or normalize compromise, those environments are functioning as provision for what you are trying to eliminate.

Run Toward the Battle

After selecting his stones, David did not wait for Goliath to approach. He ran toward him.

> *"And it came to pass, when the Philistine arose, and came and drew nigh to meet David, that David hasted, and ran toward the army to meet the Philistine."*
>
> **1 Samuel 17:48**

Preparation produces courage. And courage, when it is rooted in genuine preparation rather than emotional impulse, does not shrink from the confrontation. Many believers want dramatic deliverance without the disciplined formation that makes it sustainable. But sustained victory is not emotional, it is architectural. Victory without structure becomes a memory. Victory with structure becomes a legacy.

REFLECTION

- What disciplines have I neglected that leave me unprepared when confrontation comes?
- Am I confronting my battles emotionally or structurally?
- Where has the voice of intimidation targeted my identity?
- Have I been relying on borrowed strength instead of proven personal obedience?

APPLICATION

- Establish one daily spiritual discipline and protect it without compromise.
- Renew your mind with one Scripture that directly addresses your primary struggle.
- Strengthen one relational boundary that has been weakening your preparation.
- Identify one recurring giant and confront it from a position of covenant truth.

PRAYER

Father, prepare me before You promote me. Strengthen my private obedience and sharpen my discipline. Teach me to reject borrowed armor and rely on the faithfulness that You have built in me through the quiet places. Train my mind to resist intimidation and my spirit to run toward what You have called me to face. I choose preparation over panic. In Jesus' name, Amen.

DECLARATION: ***I am prepared. I am disciplined. I confront from covenant. I govern my mind. I build structure for sustained victory. No pigs allowed!***

CHAPTER FIVE
THE STRUGGLE

Understanding the War Within

"For the good that I would I do not: but the evil which I would not, that I do."
Romans 7:19

Not every battle is external. Some of the fiercest conflicts in the life of a believer occur entirely beneath the surface, in the interior space where desire wars against conviction, where the pull of what is familiar conflicts with the call of what is holy, and where the person you are fighting to become wrestles with the person you have spent years being. After exposure, after alignment, after preparation, many believers are surprised to discover that struggle still exists. Psychologists label this as cognitive dissonance, which is the internal or mental tension a person feels because of holding conflicting beliefs, values, or desires at the same time. It is that feeling you get when your actions don't align with what you truly believe. Like knowing what's right but doing something different or wanting change but subconsciously staying in old patterns. It is that internal battle between right and wrong that will eventually push a person to resolve this conflict either by changing their behavior or adjusting their beliefs. Demonologists, on the other hand, often identify this entanglement as signs of being demon-possessed or possibly a generational curse. From their perspective, the persistent battle, the inability to break free from destructive patterns, and the overwhelming sense of heaviness point to an external spiritual influence working against a person's well-being. In this view, what appears to be simple emotional tension may be a manifestation of spiritual oppression that requires deliverance and breaking of inherited strongholds. But if I may be simplistic, I'd like to title this as 'A struggle.' According to Webster's Dictionary, the term struggle is defined as "to make strenuous or violent efforts in the face of difficulties or opposition." This term embodies the rigorous effort required to become untethered. Every struggle is accompanied by strongholds. A stronghold is something that has a firm grip on your mind, emotions, or spirit, something that keeps you bound. This is attributed to the reason why you can't shake that thing that you are dealing with. Like the two men previously mentioned in Matthew Chapter 8, there will be times in your life when you too will be overcome with things that appear stronger than you.

Your religious affiliation does not exempt you from having a struggle. You may assume that once truth was embraced and structure was established, resistance would simply dissolve. But Scripture never promises the absence of internal conflict. It promises strength within it. Paul's confession in Romans 7 is one of the most honest passages in all his writing, and one of the most theologically important. This is not the language of spiritual immaturity. Paul wrote this from experience, from a genuine encounter with the tension that every serious believer navigates. This is the language of war. And the first thing he tells us is that the struggle does not mean you are faithless. It means you are aware. There is a profound difference between living in sin and fighting against it. One is agreement. The other is resistance. And God honors the resistance.

The Already and the Not Yet

One of the most important theological frameworks for understanding persistent struggle is the concept theologians call the already and the not yet. In Christ, something has already been accomplished that is absolute and irreversible. The old nature was crucified. Sin's dominion was broken. The penalty of guilt was paid in full. These are settled realities, not aspirations, not potentialities, not future possibilities. They are present facts about every person who is genuinely in Christ. And yet, experience tells a different story. The patterns that should be dead still stir. The flesh that should have no authority still speaks. The freedom that is already secured in the heavenly places is not yet fully manifested in the daily experience of the believer who is still living in a body shaped by years of former habits, in a world that presses against the spirit, and in a battle that requires active participation to navigate. This tension between the already and the not yet is not evidence that salvation failed. It is the normal experience of a believer who is living in the middle of a process that will not be fully complete until glory.

Understanding this does not lower the standard. It clarifies the mechanism. You do not fight for freedom as though you do not have it. You fight for freedom as though it is already real, because it is, while acknowledging that the full experience of what is already true requires ongoing cooperation with the Spirit's sanctifying work. Repentance is not the act of earning your way back to God's favor. It is the act of realigning your daily experience with a reality that God has already established. You are not trying to become free. You are learning to live in freedom you already possess. This distinction transforms the relationship with struggle. When struggle is understood as evidence that you are not truly free, it produces shame and despair. When struggle is understood as the normal friction of a person who is genuinely free learning to walk in that freedom within the constraints of a body and a world that have not yet been fully redeemed, it produces something very different, a sober, determined, grace-sustained persistence that refuses to quit and refuses to pretend, but presses forward from a position of identity rather than aspiration.

Understanding the Competing Forces

The struggle reveals competing influences within the believer. The flesh, with its deep, trained desire for comfort, familiarity, and immediate relief, presses in one direction. The spirit, renewed and inhabited by God, presses in another.

> *"For the flesh lusteth against the Spirit, and the Spirit against the flesh: and these are contrary the one to the other...",* **Galatians 5:17**

This opposition is not imaginary and ignoring it does not eliminate it. Many failures in the life of a believer are not rooted in a desire for destruction. They are rooted in a desire for relief. The flesh seeks relief quickly, familiarly, and on its own terms. The spirit seeks transformation steadily, through surrender, through the slow process of sanctification that does not yield results on a convenient timeline.

If your formative years were shaped by chaos, then peace can initially feel unfamiliar, even threatening. If your earliest coping mechanisms were developed in dysfunction, then holiness can feel restrictive before it feels freeing. The nervous system remembers what is familiar. The soul gravitates toward what it has rehearsed. This is not an excuse for continued bondage. It is an explanation that makes the path to freedom more honest and therefore more navigable. You need to understand your struggle before you can govern it.

PPLICATION

Identify one environmental trigger and take a decisive step to remove access to it.

Replace one destructive coping mechanism with a disciplined spiritual alternative.

Memorize Romans 6:11 and rehearse it audibly during moments of temptation.

Establish a daily renewal practice combining Scripture, prayer, and accountability.

PRAYER

Father, strengthen me in the struggle. Teach me to mortify what weakens me and renew what strengthens me. Remove shame and replace it with discipline rooted in grace. Help me recognize the triggers that open doors and reject agreements I have made with the flesh. I choose sanctification over surrender. In Jesus' name, Amen.

DECLARATION

I am not my struggle. I am renewed daily.
I mortify the flesh through the Spirit.
I refuse the return narrative.
I fight under grace.
No pigs allowed!

The Root System of Recurring Struggle

Recurring struggle is rarely about a single moment of weakness. It has a root system, a network of contributing factors that feed the pattern and sustain its power. When the same struggle returns despite genuine repentance and sincere effort, it is worth asking more carefully: What environment reinforces it? What narrative justifies it? What emotion most consistently triggers it? What agreement sustains it beneath the level of conscious awareness?

These are excavation questions. They require more than a quick prayer and a renewed commitment. They require the kind of honest, sustained examination that most people avoid because it is uncomfortable, and because what it uncovers forces a confrontation with parts of the story they have carefully arranged not to look at too directly.

> *"For if ye live after the flesh, ye shall die: but if ye through the Spirit do mortify the deeds of the body, ye shall live."* **Romans 8:13**

Mortification is one of the most neglected concepts in contemporary discipleship. It does not mean suppression or pushing the struggle underground, where it continues to operate out of sight. It rather means intentional weakening. It means systematically removing the supply lines that feed what you are trying to eliminate. You cannot starve what you continue to feed. Every time you return to the environment that reinforces the pattern, you are feeding it. Every time you entertain the narrative that justifies it, you are feeding it. Every time you choose the familiar relief over the uncomfortable obedience, you are feeding it. And what you feed will grow.

Shame Is Not the Answer

One of the greatest obstacles in the journey through struggle is the role of shame. Shame paralyzes. It rehearses failure without pointing toward freedom. It defines identity by the struggle rather than by the grace that is available within it. The believer who is drowning in shame over a recurring pattern often cannot access the very resources that would help them overcome it, because shame convinces them that those resources are not available to someone who keeps failing in the same place. Shame and conviction are not the same thing. Conviction is the Holy Spirit saying: this is not who you are, this is not who you are called to be, and here is the grace to move in a different direction. Shame is the enemy saying: this is

exactly who you are, this is all you will ever be, and there in trying again. One is the voice of God. The other is not.

> *"Likewise reckon ye also yourselves to be dead ind unto sin, but alive unto God through Jesus Christ Lord."* **Romans 6:11**

Reckon means consider it settled. Not emotionally settled, s settled. You are not your struggle. You are engaged in a wa it. And that war is already being fought from a position because of what Christ accomplished on your behalf. The st real. But so is your authority in Christ. And surrender is choice.

REFLECTION

- What emotion most consistently precedes my struggle?
- Have I mistaken the familiarity of a pattern for part of my identity?
- Where has shame been silencing my progress rather than conviction guiding it?
- Am I mortifying the flesh intentionally, or merely managi on the surface?

The Root System of Recurring Struggle

Recurring struggle is rarely about a single moment of weakness. It has a root system, a network of contributing factors that feed the pattern and sustain its power. When the same struggle returns despite genuine repentance and sincere effort, it is worth asking more carefully: What environment reinforces it? What narrative justifies it? What emotion most consistently triggers it? What agreement sustains it beneath the level of conscious awareness?

These are excavation questions. They require more than a quick prayer and a renewed commitment. They require the kind of honest, sustained examination that most people avoid because it is uncomfortable, and because what it uncovers forces a confrontation with parts of the story they have carefully arranged not to look at too directly.

> *"For if ye live after the flesh, ye shall die: but if ye through the Spirit do mortify the deeds of the body, ye shall live."* **Romans 8:13**

Mortification is one of the most neglected concepts in contemporary discipleship. It does not mean suppression or pushing the struggle underground, where it continues to operate out of sight. It rather means intentional weakening. It means systematically removing the supply lines that feed what you are trying to eliminate. You cannot starve what you continue to feed. Every time you return to the environment that reinforces the pattern, you are feeding it. Every time you entertain the narrative that justifies it, you are feeding it. Every time you choose the familiar relief over the uncomfortable obedience, you are feeding it. And what you feed will grow.

Shame Is Not the Answer

One of the greatest obstacles in the journey through struggle is the role of shame. Shame paralyzes. It rehearses failure without pointing toward freedom. It defines identity by the struggle rather than by the grace that is available within it. The believer who is drowning in shame over a recurring pattern often cannot access the very resources that would help them overcome it, because shame convinces them that those resources are not available to someone who keeps failing in the same place. Shame and conviction are not the same thing. Conviction is the Holy Spirit saying: this is not who you are, this is not who you are called to be, and here is the grace to move in a different direction. Shame is the enemy saying: this is exactly who you are, this is all you will ever be, and there is no point in trying again. One is the voice of God. The other is not.

> *"Likewise reckon ye also yourselves to be dead indeed unto sin, but alive unto God through Jesus Christ our Lord."* **Romans 6:11**

Reckon means consider it settled. Not emotionally settled, spiritually settled. You are not your struggle. You are engaged in a war against it. And that war is already being fought from a position of victory because of what Christ accomplished on your behalf. The struggle is real. But so is your authority in Christ. And surrender is always a choice.

REFLECTION

- What emotion most consistently precedes my struggle?
- Have I mistaken the familiarity of a pattern for part of my identity?
- Where has shame been silencing my progress rather than conviction guiding it?
- Am I mortifying the flesh intentionally, or merely managing it on the surface?

APPLICATION

- Identify one environmental trigger and take a decisive step to remove access to it.
- Replace one destructive coping mechanism with a disciplined spiritual alternative.
- Memorize Romans 6:11 and rehearse it audibly during moments of temptation.
- Establish a daily renewal practice combining Scripture, prayer, and accountability.

PRAYER

Father, strengthen me in the struggle. Teach me to mortify what weakens me and renew what strengthens me. Remove shame and replace it with discipline rooted in grace. Help me recognize the triggers that open doors and reject agreements I have made with the flesh. I choose sanctification over surrender. In Jesus' name, Amen.

DECLARATION

I am not my struggle. I am renewed daily.
I mortify the flesh through the Spirit.
I refuse the return narrative.
I fight under grace.
No pigs allowed!

SECTION III

SABOTEURS

Recognizing the Enemies Within

— — —

Not every enemy stands outside the gate. Some opposition is internal. Some sabotage is self-generated. Some collapse begins not with an external attack but with a quiet permission granted from within, a wound that was never addressed, a pride that was never examined, a door that was left open not through dramatic rebellion but through casual indifference.

This section confronts the quiet adversaries, the attitudes, postures, and permissions that undermine progress from within the heart. These are the saboteurs that coexist with genuine faith, that attend church alongside sincere devotion, and that operate beneath the threshold of what the people around you can see. If the territory has been exposed and the roots excavated, now vigilance must sharpen. Because what is not guarded will be reentered. Saboteurs thrive where governance weakens.

CHAPTER SIX

THE SPIRIT OF ABSALOM

When Pride Seeks the Throne

"And Absalom said moreover,
Oh that I were made judge in the land, that every
man which hath any suit or cause might come unto
me, and I would do him justice!"
2 Samuel 15:4

Not every enemy stands outside your life. Some opposition forms within the heart, cultivated quietly over time, nourished by wounds that were never healed and ambitions that were never surrendered. After exposure, excavation, and honest confrontation with personal struggle, a more subtle danger must be addressed. It is not open rebellion. It is quite an ambition. It is not loud defiance. It is concealed resentment operating beneath a veneer of competence and apparent loyalty.

The spirit of Absalom is not merely a historical account from the court of King David. It is a living pattern, a recurring spiritual anatomy that appears in homes, churches, workplaces, and ministries wherever wounded pride is given permission to operate unchecked. Understanding it is not optional for the serious believer. It is essential, because this spirit is one of the most effective saboteurs in the kingdom of God, and it almost always begins with something that feels entirely justified.

Generational Patterns and the Responsibility to Break Them

Absalom's story does not begin with Absalom. It begins with David, with the fractures in David's household that created the environment in which the spirit of Absalom could take root and flourish. David's sin with Bathsheba, his failure to address Amnon's violation of Tamar, his inconsistency as a father, these created a relational landscape of unresolved injustice, unaddressed pain, and unacknowledged dysfunction that Absalom inherited. He was, in a very real sense, the product of a broken generational context that was never properly healed. This is not presented as an excuse for Absalom's choices. He was accountable for what he did with what he received. But it is presented as a sobering reality about the nature of generational patterns: what one generation fails to address, the next generation inherits and often amplifies. The violence that David initiated in the Uriah affair escalated in the household. The pride that went unchecked in the father reappeared with greater destructive force in the son. Patterns do not simply disappear between generations. They go underground, and they surface in the next generation with the accumulated energy of everything that was never confronted.

Scripture acknowledges this reality with striking directness. The principle of visiting iniquity upon the children of those who reject God is not a statement of divine cruelty. It is a description of how unaddressed generational sin operates. Broken patterns of behavior, damaged relational templates, unhealed wounds, and entrenched cycles of dysfunction pass from parent to child not through genetics alone but through modeling, environment, and the subtle transmission of unresolved spiritual agreements. Children learn what they live. They absorb the emotional and spiritual climate of their homes far more deeply than most parents realize. But, and this is the heart of the gospel's power over generational bondage, cycles can be broken. The trajectory of a family line can be redirected. What has been passed down does not have to be passed on. Galatians 3:13 declares that Christ has redeemed us from the curse of the law. That redemption is not limited to personal sin. It extends to the generational patterns that have shaped the soil of your life. You have been chosen, in this generation, in this moment, to be the person who says: this pattern stops here. It will not continue through me. I am not the continuation of what was broken. I am the beginning of what God is restoring.

Who Absalom Was

Absalom was the third son of King David. His name, Avshalom in Hebrew, means "father of peace", one of the more tragic ironies in Scripture, given that his life produced war, division, betrayal, and the near destruction of his father's kingdom. He was remarkable in appearance, magnetic in personality, and extraordinarily gifted in leadership. The Scripture says of him that from the sole of his foot to the crown of his head there was no blemish in him. He had access.

He had proximity. He had every advantage that position and relationship could offer.

But beneath the gifts and the beauty lay a heart that had never fully healed. His sister Tamar had been violated by his half-brother Amnon. David, his father, knew what had happened and did nothing. Absalom's grief and rage, understandable, legitimate in origin, were left to fester without resolution, without justice, without the healing conversation that should have happened but never did. And over two years of silence, that wound became something else. It became a narrative. It became an identity. It became a permission slip for rebellion.

How the Spirit Operates

Absalom positioned himself at the city gate, the place of influence, the access point between the people and rightful authority. And there he listened. He sympathized. He validated grievances. He offered the appearance of understanding and justice. But notice what he was not doing: he was not directing people toward healing. He was not promoting reconciliation. He was not building alignment. He was cultivating allegiance to himself.

"So Absalom stole the hearts of the men of Israel." **2 Samuel 15:6**

The word "stole" is significant. He did not earn these hearts through genuine service and proven integrity. He appropriated them through the strategic use of sympathy and the exploitation of unresolved grievances. This is the anatomy of the Absalom spirit: it validates without healing, sympathizes without reconciling, and creates emotional agreement that is ultimately redirected toward self-exaltation rather than covenant alignment. Pride rarely announces itself as pride. It disguises itself as discernment. It convinces you that you see what others do not, that the authority over you is inadequate, that if you were in charge things would be different, that the system is flawed but you are the solution. It does not feel like rebellion. It feels like clarity. And that is precisely what makes it so dangerous.

The Root of Bitterness

Every Absalom spirit has its origin in unhealed offense. David's failure to address the wound in his family created the soil in which Absalom's rebellion took root and grew. This is a sobering reality for parents, leaders, and anyone in a position of spiritual authority:

unaddressed wounds in the people entrusted to your care do not simply disappear. They go underground. And underground wounds, left to develop in darkness, can grow into something that surfaces with devastating force.

> *"Looking diligently lest any man fail of the grace of God; lest any root of bitterness springing up trouble you, and thereby many be defiled."* **Hebrews 12:15**

Roots grow beneath the surface before they disturb what is visible. Sabotage begins internally long before it manifests externally. If there is stored resentment in your heart, I mean, a narrative you rehearse about how you were wronged, a wound that has never been brought into the open and offered to God for healing, it is functioning as a root of bitterness. And roots of bitterness, if not addressed, will eventually produce fruit that defiles not only you but the people around you.

Defeating the Spirit of Absalom

Absalom's death was both tragic and theologically precise. He was riding on a mule, fleeing from the battle that his own ambition had produced, when his head was caught in the branches of a great oak.

He was left suspended between heaven and earth, unable to advance, unable to retreat, held by the very thing he had gloried in. His long hair, the symbol of his pride and the object of his vanity, became his trap.

This is the testimony of every Absalom spirit: it is ultimately suspended by its own glory. Pride without submission does not ascend, it hangs. And the way this spirit is defeated in your own life follows the same pattern. It dies when pride is dethroned. It loses its power when humility is genuinely embraced, not as a performance but as a settled conviction. It is overcome when you choose submission over self-exaltation, correction over justification, and alignment over ambition. The throne belongs to God alone, and the spirit of Absalom is defeated the moment you stop trying to claim what is not yours to occupy.

REFLECTION

- Is there unresolved offense quietly influencing my perception of people in authority?
- Do I resist correction more readily than I receive it?
- Have I elevated my own perspective above proper alignment?

- Where might pride be seeking subtle control in my relationships or calling?

APPLICATION

- Identify any unresolved resentment and bring it honestly before God in prayer.
- Invite correction in one area where you notice defensiveness rising.
- Examine whether your current ambitions are aligned with obedience or competing with it.
- Pray specifically for a spirit of genuine humility and rightful alignment.

PRAYER

Father, guard my heart from pride. Expose any hidden resentment or quiet ambition that seeks control apart from Your will. Teach me genuine humility, not as a performance but as a posture. Keep me properly aligned under rightful authority. Let my influence always flow from submission, not from self-exaltation. In Jesus' name, Amen.

I reject pride.

I embrace humility.

I remain aligned.

I receive correction.

I guard my heart from internal sabotage.

No pigs allowed!

CHAPTER SEVEN
THE GARAGE DOOR
When Access Is Quietly Granted

"Neither give place to the devil." **Ephesians 4:27**

Not all sabotage is dramatic. Some of it is casual. There are moments in life when the front door remains locked, the windows are secured, and everything visible appears intact, but the garage door has been quietly left open. From the street everything looks safe. Nothing appears compromised. Yet access has been granted. I want to share a personal experience that gave this chapter its life while I was still writing it. Like most people, I use my garage daily and give it very little thought. One evening I came home to find the garage door wide open. A family member had come through earlier and left it open without realizing it. A few days passed. When I opened the garage to take my son to swim class, things had fallen from the storage shelf and parts of the space were in disarray. Then, out of the corner of my eye, I caught something furry dart across the floor. I looked beneath the car, beneath the shelves, nothing. I assumed I had imagined it and moved on with the day.

That same night, I went to get a drink of water, and the creature appeared again, darting under the car, fast and panicked. My heart raced. My mind immediately went to practical questions: What is this? How long has it been here? How do I remove it without making things worse? I considered simply shutting and locking the garage door, but I quickly recognized the problem with that approach: locking the door with the intruder inside does not solve the problem. It only changes where the problem lives. I called a professional. The resolution was effective but costly, $432 and days of disruption, all because a door was left open.

The Cost of Carelessness

One of the most important lessons embedded in the garage door story is the disproportionate relationship between the size of the oversight and the scale of the consequence. The door was left open by a family member, casually, without intention, without malice. Nobody decided that the house should be exposed to whatever wandered in from outside. It simply was not thought about carefully enough in that moment. And yet the consequence was weeks of disruption, significant financial cost, and a level of stress and inconvenience that far exceeded anything that the brief moment of carelessness seemed to warrant.

Spiritual carelessness operates by the same disproportionate mathematics. The access point that produces the most lasting damage is rarely dramatic. It is rarely the result of a deliberate choice to rebel. It is the unguarded moment, the casual exception to a usually maintained standard, the "just this once" that never actually stays just once. The enemy does not require a large opening. He is extraordinarily efficient with small ones. A small and consistent access point, maintained over months or years, can produce damage that looks entirely out of proportion to the size of the permission that was granted. This is why Proverbs 4:23 commands us to (guard the heart) with all diligence, not some diligence, not reasonable diligence, not diligence that is proportional to how dramatic the threat appears. All diligence. Because from the heart flow the issues of life. Everything downstream, decisions, relationships, habits, trajectory, legacy, is affected by what happens at the level of the heart. And the heart is guarded not primarily through dramatic spiritual warfare in moments of obvious crisis, but through the consistent, unglamorous practice of maintaining the everyday disciplines that keep access points sealed.

When I paid $432 to remove that animal from my garage, I was not only paying for the removal. I was paying for the weeks of undisturbed habitation. I was paying for the damage that had already been done while I was unaware. I was paying for the disruption to my peace, my routine, and my family's sense of security in their own space. The cost of allowing an intruder to remain is always greater than the cost of preventing their entry in the first place. This is as true in the spiritual domain as it is in the natural one. Vigilance is always less expensive than recovery.

What the Garage Door Represents

I have told that story in several settings and watched people recognize themselves in it immediately. Because most of us have a garage door somewhere in our lives. Not a literal one, a spiritual, emotional, or behavioral one. An access point that is not obviously open and therefore does not feel urgently dangerous, but through which things enter that were never invited and cost far more than we anticipated to remove.

Spiritual vulnerability often works this way. You may reject obvious sin with genuine conviction. You may resist overt temptation with real discipline. You may maintain visible markers of serious faith. But if subtle permissions remain, if there are quiet allowances you have not yet examined, intrusion remains possible. The enemy does not need full ownership of a life to do significant damage. He only needs space. He only needs the garage door.

> *"Lest Satan should get an advantage of us: for we are not ignorant of his devices."* **2 Corinthians 2:11**

Ignorance is not innocence. It is vulnerability. His devices are strategies and patterns of exploitation that he has refined through long observation of human weakness. And the most effective strategy in his arsenal is rarely the dramatic frontal assault. It is the quiet exploitation of the door that was left open in a moment of exhaustion, grief, loneliness, or simple inattention.

The Doors We Leave Open

Doors are opened in many ways. Some are opened through deliberate rebellion and a knowing choice to step into territory that God has forbidden. But many, perhaps most, are opened through more subtle means. Unchecked fatigue lowers the defenses. Unresolved grief creates emotional vulnerability that becomes an entry point. Sustained loneliness softens standards that would otherwise hold firm. Unprocessed anger leaves interior doors ajar that are designed to be sealed.

Digital habits function as garage doors for enormous numbers of people, the casual browsing that begins innocently and drifts gradually toward content that weakens conviction. Relationships function as garage doors, the friendship that does not directly challenge you toward God but consistently normalizes compromise at a low enough level that you do not feel alarmed. Internal narratives function as garage doors, the agreement you carry with a lie about your identity or your worth that keeps a wound just open enough to be exploitable.

> *"But put ye on the Lord Jesus Christ, and make not provision for the flesh, to fulfil the lusts thereof."*
>
> **Romans 13:14**

Provision means preparation, supply, accessibility. If access remains available, then the temptation will remain convenient. You cannot simultaneously claim to resist a pattern and continue to maintain the supply lines that feed it. Removing provision is not a spiritual bonus activity for the highly disciplined believer. It is a basic requirement for anyone serious about sustained freedom.

Closing the Door and Opening a New One

The good news, and there is always good news in God, is that you are not powerless over the doors in your life. You have the authority to close what has been left open. But closing requires intentionality and honesty. It requires an inventory that goes deeper than the obvious. Ask yourself with full sincerity: What conversations reopen old narratives? What environments consistently affect your conviction? What relationships maintain access to patterns you are claiming to resist? What digital or entertainment habits function as provision for what you are trying to eliminate?

Governance begins with responsibility. You are not a passive victim of your own access points. You are accountable for what you have permitted to remain open. Accountability, when embraced honestly, is not condemnation, it is the restoration of agency. When you close a door deliberately, you are not simply removing a problem. You are making a declaration: I am the one in authority here. This is my territory. And this access is now revoked.

REFLECTION

- Where have I casually granted access that I have not yet fully examined?
- What habits or patterns create silent vulnerability in my daily life?
- Do I maintain provision for patterns I claim to be resisting?
- Are my spiritual and relational boundaries clear and firm, or are they negotiable?

APPLICATION

- Identify one area of silent access this week and close it with a deliberate decision.

- Remove one digital or environmental trigger that consistently weakens your discipline.
- Establish one non-negotiable boundary in a vulnerable area of your life.
- Invite specific accountability regarding an area where hidden permission remains.

PRAYER

Father, reveal any access I have granted unknowingly or carelessly. Strengthen my vigilance and teach me to remove every provision for the flesh. Help me build wise, strong boundaries that protect what You have restored. Guard my spirit from the kind of erosion that happens gradually and without announcement. I choose discipline over convenience. In Jesus' name, Amen.

DECLARATION

I give no place to the enemy.
I remove provision for the flesh.
I build strong boundaries.
I govern my spirit.
I guard my territory.
No pigs allowed!

SECTION IV
INTERNAL BONDAGES

Untying the Soul and Restoring Alignment

— — —

Freedom from behavior does not always mean freedom within. You can change what you do on the outside and still carry significant bondage on the inside. You can close visible doors and still feel the pull of what lies behind them. Attachment can entangle what discipline alone cannot break. Emotional alignment outside covenant order can bind the soul more deeply than any behavioral pattern.

This section addresses the relational and internal bondages that are rarely discussed in the context of deliverance, the soul ties that distort identity, the fragmentation that follows repeated cycles of sin and shame, and the path toward genuine wholeness that goes deeper than behavior modification. What you join yourself to shapes you. What you carry in your soul influences every decision you make. Covenant language matters. Alignment must be restored before freedom can fully mature.

CHAPTER EIGHT
SOUL TIES

When Attachment Becomes Entanglement

"Know ye not that he which is joined to an harlot is one body? for two, saith he, shall be one flesh."
1 Corinthians 6:16

Freedom from behavior does not always mean freedom within. You can close doors and still feel pulled toward what was behind them. You can establish new disciplines and still sense the gravitational weight of former attachments. You can remove access and still experience a kind of internal entanglement that discipline alone seems unable to fully resolve. This is the territory of soul ties, and it is territory that the church has often been too uncomfortable to discuss with the clarity and theological depth it requires. The concept of a soul tie is not mystical exaggeration. It is a recognition of a biblical reality: that human beings are not merely physical creatures who happen to have an interior life. We are deeply relational, and our relationships, especially those that involve significant intimacy, shared spiritual experience, or formative emotional intensity, leave marks on the soul that do not simply disappear when the relationship ends.

What You Join Yourself to Shapes You

The principle of soul ties rests on a foundational theological truth that runs consistently through Scripture: human beings are profoundly shaped by what they attach themselves to. This shaping is not superficial. It is not merely behavioral or habitual. It reaches into the deepest registers of identity, affecting how you see yourself, how you interpret reality, what you expect from relationships, and what you believe is possible for your life. The soul is not a sealed container that remains unchanged by its associations. It is permeable, responsive, and formative. It takes on the character of what it consistently dwells in. This is why Scripture is so specific about relational boundaries. It is not because God is restrictive or suspicious of human connection. It is because God understands the mechanics of the soul better than we do, and He knows that the connections we form do not simply provide companionship or enjoyment, they provide formation. You become, in meaningful ways, like what you consistently expose yourself to. The person whose closest relationships are governed by wisdom and covenant will find their own wisdom and covenant-mindedness reinforced and deepened. The person whose closest associations are with those who normalize compromise will find their own standards quietly softening over time, often without consciously noticing the shift.

Proverbs 13:20 states this plainly: he who walks with wise men will be wise, but the companion of fools will suffer harm. This is not a statement about the moral superiority of one group of people over another. It is a description of how association produces formation. Wisdom is transmitted through proximity. So is foolishness. And when the attachment runs deep, when it has reached the level of a soul tie, the formation that it produces is correspondingly deep. Removing the relationship does not automatically remove the formation that the relationship produced. That is why breaking a soul tie requires more than simply ending a connection. It requires the active dismantling of the identity it created and the intentional rebuilding of a truer one.

The Covenantal Design of Union

Scripture teaches consistently that joining produces consequence. This is not presented as a warning against closeness or intimacy; it is a description of how human beings are designed to function. Union is covenantal in Scripture. It is not casual, not neutral, and not without lasting effect.

> *"Therefore shall a man leave his father and his mother, and shall cleave unto his wife: and they shall be one flesh."* **Genesis 2:24**

The word "cleave" in Hebrew carries the meaning of adhesion and it means to bind firmly, to attach in a way that is not easily reversed. God designed this capacity for covenant union as something beautiful. In the context of marriage, it produces strength, stability, and the kind of deep knowing that builds across a lifetime. In the context of godly friendship, as seen in the relationship of David and Jonathan, it creates bonds of loyalty and mutual investment that transcend circumstance. These are positive soul ties, the kind that make you stronger, more whole, more aligned with who God created you to be. But the same capacity for covenant union that produces blessing in its proper context produces entanglement in improper contexts. When covenant behavior occurs outside covenant order, when sexual intimacy is shared outside marriage, when emotional dependencies are formed with people who operate outside God's purposes for your life, when shared spiritual experiences create attachment to what should be released, attachment forms without divine alignment. The result is a soul tie that distorts rather than strengthens. It pulls rather than propels.

Trauma and Soul Ties

Not all soul ties are formed through relationships. Some are formed through experiences, particularly traumatic ones. Trauma creates a kind of soul tie with the moment of injury that keeps the past perpetually present. A sound, a tone of voice, a specific smell, a particular environment can trigger a return to the pain of the original wound with a vividness that feels entirely immediate. The body remembers. The soul remembers. And what was supposed to be history continues to function as present reality. These trauma-based ties are often connected to the trigger patterns that believers struggle to explain. You respond with disproportionate fear to a situation that others navigate calmly because your soul is still tethered to the moment when that kind of situation first becomes dangerous. You withdraw from a particular kind of relationship not because of current evidence, but because of what a former relationship taught you to expect. These are not signs of weakness. They are signs of unhealed attachment that needs to be addressed with both spiritual intentionality and compassionate honesty.

Breaking Ungodly Soul Ties

The process of breaking ungodly soul ties begins with honest recognition. You must acknowledge the connection, name it, assess its influence, and understand how it has been affecting your obedience, your identity, and your spiritual clarity. Denial does not weaken a soul tie. It only ensures that its influence continues beneath the threshold of your awareness. From recognition, the process moves to prayer and repentance, specifically asking God to sever every illegal, unauthorized, and covenant-violating connection. This is not a one-time formula. It is the beginning of a spiritual process of reorientation that may require sustained prayer, wise counsel, and patient trust in God's ability to restore what has been fragmented. *"If a man therefore purge himself from these, he shall be a vessel unto honour, sanctified, and meet for the master's use..."* **2 Timothy 2:21**

Purging is not cruelty. It is preparation. The difficulty in releasing some attachments is real and should not be minimized. When something has been formative in your identity, releasing it feels like losing a part of yourself. But what feels like loss is actually the beginning of recovery. You are not losing who you are; you are recovering who God made you to be before the entanglement rewrote the story. Untying the soul does not mean abandoning love. It means restoring order. It means conforming your relational architecture to the image of the One you were designed to reflect.

REFLECTION

- Is there an attachment, maybe a person, an experience, or a pattern that consistently influences my obedience?
- Have I confused emotional intensity or familiarity with covenant alignment?
- Where has loyalty to a person or relationship replaced my discernment?
- What tie needs to be honestly examined and, where necessary, severed?

APPLICATION

- Identify one relationship that currently weakens your spiritual clarity and establish clear boundaries.
- Seek wise counsel before making any significant decisions in areas of emotional entanglement.
- Pray specifically and persistently for covenant realignment in vulnerable areas.
- Remove one physical reminder that continues to reinforce an unhealthy attachment.

PRAYER

Father, reveal any attachment that distorts my obedience or clouds my identity in You. Give me the courage to realign where necessary, even when it is painful. Untie what binds me outside of Your order. Strengthen my identity in Christ above every emotional influence. I choose covenant alignment over entanglement. In Jesus' name, Amen.

DECLARATION

I am aligned with covenant truth.
I release every unhealthy attachment.
I guard my identity in Christ. I walk in discernment.
I choose alignment over entanglement.
No pigs allowed.

CHAPTER NINE
WHOLENESS

When Alignment Becomes Integration

"Unite my heart to fear thy name." **Psalm 86:11**

Freedom is not the final goal. Wholeness is. You can be delivered from a pattern and still feel fragmented. You can break a soul tie and still feel internally divided. You can establish boundaries and still sense an inconsistency between who you are in your private moments and who you present yourself to be in your public ones. Deliverance removes what does not belong.

Deliverance is real, and when God sets you free, the chains truly do fall off. Yet there are moments when, even after stepping into freedom, you still carry the residue or the trails of bondage of the things that once held you. Residue doesn't mean you're not delivered;

it simply reflects that your soul is still adjusting to a new reality. It's the faint imprint of where bondage once existed, the subtle reactions, thoughts, or insecurities that rise not because you're still bound, but because you're healing from what being bound once taught you. It is the afterglow of an old season trying to echo in a new one. But residue is not a verdict; it's an invitation. An invitation for God to continue cleansing, renewing, and reshaping you as you walk out your freedom day by day. Over time, the residue fades, the trails disappear, and your identity becomes fully aligned with the freedom you already possess.

Wholeness restores what was never meant to be absent.

During the formation of this chapter, I can recall dealing with the feeling of inadequacy and brokenness resulting from the absence of a father in my life. I grew up many years despising him because of his absence. At the heart of the matter was the question of why my father left us, or why he became obsolete during my formative years. For years, I struggled with unanswered questions regarding why I was among the many young men who were raised in a single-parent home. I even tried to convince myself that growing up without a father was more beneficial for me. When asked questions regarding who he was, what he did, and why he was not a part of my life? The answers would often result in lies. I can recall describing him as a professional individual who had a plethora of distinct occupations. He was a medical doctor, a lawyer, and even an intellectual teacher who took good care of his family and provided a strong image for his sons. All of this was an absolute lie! The truth is I vaguely remembered him, had no relationship with him, and wasn't sure if he was dead or alive. I somehow blamed him for many of the issues that I got into. Like many of us, I convinced myself that if my father had played an active role in my life, I would have been a better person. If my father was a part of my life, I would not have entangled myself in some of the things that I did growing up. This absence of a father in my life propelled me to figure out manhood on my own. I learned manhood through trial and error. I was broken and blamed him for many blunders that I caused in my early years. Blunders that caused me to invite "pigs" in my life. Disguised anger, hatred, unforgiveness, bitterness, and even mistrust. If you can identify with any of the previously mentioned "pigs", you too have broken areas in your life that need to be mended.

We don't realize that one bad seed sown in our lives will eventually sprout into a huge unhealthy tree that will take years to remove. Things we picked up as a child on the journey of life will reside in our barns and create other areas of brokenness. It took me years of making wrong decisions and using poor judgment before I concluded that growing up without a father did not define who I was. He made the choice to be absent from my life, and I had to release him for his ignorance. Get to the place where you can now assume responsibility for the things you got yourself into and get on the journey to wholeness.

The truth is many people struggle with things such as; inadequacy, low self-esteem, and low self-worth, anxiety, anger, and fear. Those are just symptoms. However, you must get to the source. You have not experienced complete wholeness because you have only treated some of the symptoms and never address the source. Few are willing to go deep enough to confront the source. It's easier to correct surface-level behaviors than to dig into the root that gives birth to those actions. We often medicate our pain with temporary fixes; new habits, affirmations, or distractions, and approval from people who need validation themselves. But those only soothe the symptoms for a while. Until the root is exposed and dealt with, the symptoms will continue to reappear in different forms. Your behavior is simply the evidence that you might be delivered but lack wholeness.

The psalmist's prayer in Psalm 86:11 assumes something profoundly important: the heart can become divided. That is not the language of irredeemable brokenness, it is an honest recognition of what sin, trauma, and misaligned attachment do to the interior life of a human being. They fragment. They compartmentalize. They create a soul that is operating in multiple registers simultaneously, with different parts pulling in different directions, allegiances divided, convictions competing with impulses, the person you want to be at war with the person your history has made.

The Practical Process of Integration

Wholeness does not arrive as a single experience. It is the cumulative result of many smaller integrations, moments when what was previously compartmentalized is brought into the light, examined, surrendered to God, and allowed to be reinterpreted through the lens of His purposes. Each of these moments contributes to the gradual reconstruction of an interior life that is increasingly unified in its allegiance, increasingly stable in its identity, and increasingly capable of the sustained, fruitful living that God designed.

The process begins with honesty, a willingness to acknowledge the places where fragmentation exists rather than papering over them with spiritual language. Many believers have become proficient at describing their inner experience in ways that sound like wholeness without inhabiting it. They use the right vocabulary, the right declarations, the right confessions. But beneath the language, the compartmentalization remains. The outer life presents one story, and the interior life tells another. Wholeness requires the courage to close that gap, to bring the inner reality into alignment with the outer declaration, not by pretending the inner reality is better than it is, but by genuinely engaging the process of transformation that makes the declaration true.

The second element of the integration process is grief, the willingness to mourn what was lost or damaged without allowing that mourning to become the defining story. Many people skip the grief stage in their pursuit of freedom and wonder why the wholeness they seek remains elusive. Grief is not weakness. It is the honest acknowledgement of real loss, the years that were spent in bondage, the relationships that were damaged, the opportunities that were missed, the version of yourself that you never fully became because of what was living in your life without permission. These losses are real, and they deserve to be mourned. But mourning is meant to be passed through, not lived in. It is the valley, not the destination.

The third element is reinterpretation, allowing God to give meaning to what seemed meaningless, purpose to what seemed wasted, and redemption to what seemed irredeemable. This is precisely what Joseph did in Genesis 50 when he told his brothers that what they intended for evil, God had meant for good. He did not deny the harm. He did not minimize the years of suffering. He reinterpreted them through the framework of divine sovereignty, and in doing so, found a wholeness that transcended his history. This is the kind of integration that produces genuine peace, not the absence of a painful past, but the presence of a God who has already determined how to redeem it.

The Theology of Fragmentation

Fragmentation does not typically occur through a single catastrophic event. It develops gradually, through repeated experiences that teach the soul to separate what should be integrated. When you sin and then attend worship without repentance, a division forms between your spiritual exterior and your internal reality. When you are wounded and choose numbness over grief, a division forms between your emotional truth and the version of yourself you allow others to see. When you hold contradictory beliefs, knowing what Scripture says but operating from a different set of assumptions in practice, a division forms between your stated theology and your functional one.

Compartmentalization is the soul's strategy for surviving what it cannot yet process. It allows functioning to continue when integration is too painful. But compartmentalization is a coping mechanism, not a solution. It preserves survival at the cost of integrity, and integrity, at its root, simply means wholeness: the state in which the inner and outer life agree.

> *"A double minded man is unstable in all his ways."* ,
>
> **James 1:8**

Double mindedness produces instability because allegiance is divided. When you are attempting to move in two directions simultaneously, progress in either direction is compromised. The double-minded person is not a bad person. They are divided ones.

And division, of allegiance, of identity, of purpose, is the enemy of the fruitful, stable life that God intends for every believer.

Sanctification Is the Spirit's Reconstruction Work

Wholeness is not a destination you arrive at after sufficient effort. It is the Spirit's ongoing work of reconstruction, the steady, patient, sometimes slow process of integrating what was fragmented, healing what was wounded, and conforming the whole person to the image of Christ. It is what the Scripture calls sanctification.

> *"And the very God of peace sanctify you wholly; and I pray God your whole spirit and soul and body be preserved blameless unto the coming of our Lord Jesus Christ."* **1 Thessalonians 5:23**

Wholly. Not partially. Not behaviorally only. The scope of God's sanctifying work is comprehensive. He does not merely adjust the outer conduct and leaves the inner life in its fragmented state. He is interested in the whole person, the spirit that relates to God, the soul that navigates relationships and carries history, and the body that lives in the physical world and acts on what the mind and spirit dictate. This work takes time. Some wounds require extended seasons to settle. Some memories require patient reframing, not the artificial positive spin of denial, but the deep interpretive work of seeing your history through the lens of divine purpose. Joseph's words to his brothers after years of betrayal, slavery, and imprisonment carry the weight of this kind of reframing:

> *"But as for you, ye thought evil against me; but God meant it unto good..."* **Genesis 50:20**

Joseph did not deny the harm that was done to him. He did not minimize the pain of the years in the pit and the prison. He interpreted them through the lens of divine sovereignty, and in doing so, found a wholeness that transcended his history without pretending it did not exist. Healing does not rewrite history. It redeems it. That redemption is available to you.

REFLECTION

- Where do I feel internally divided, where the outer life and inner life are not yet in agreement?
- Is shame still influencing my identity more than the truth of who I am in Christ?

- Have I allowed memory to define me more powerfully than the Word of God?
- Am I renewing my mind intentionally and consistently?

APPLICATION

- Identify one specific area where inner and outer life feel misaligned and bring it honestly to God.
- Meditate on 2 Corinthians 5:17 daily for one month as an anchor for your identity.
- Establish consistent abiding practices, prayer, Scripture, and community, as the architecture of wholeness.
- Seek wise counsel if fragmentation has been persistent and deeply rooted.

PRAYER

Father, unite my heart. Where I have been divided, bring integration. Where shame lingers, replace it with the settled identity of what it means to be Yours. Sanctify me wholly: spirit, soul, and body. Renew my mind daily and teach me to abide in You consistently. I choose alignment and wholeness. In Jesus' name, Amen.

DECLARATION

My heart is united.

I am sanctified wholly.

I abide in Christ.

I reject shame.

I walk in wholeness.

No pigs allowed!

SECTION V

VIGILANCE

Managing Post-Deliverance Vulnerability

— — —

Victory is not the end of vulnerability. This is a truth that most people are not prepared for when they first experience genuine deliverance, and the unpreparedness itself becomes a form of danger. After breakthrough comes quiet. After deliverance comes routine. After restoration comes the normalcy of ordinary days that do not feel spiritually charged or urgently significant. And it is often in that normalcy, in the unremarkable middle of a season that feels stable, that vigilance fades.

Relapse is rarely explosive. It is cumulative. Drift precedes collapse. The house that was swept clean does not typically get reoccupied through a single catastrophic decision. It gets reoccupied through the gradual loosening of disciplines, the slow normalization of small compromises, and the quiet permission granted to things that should have been refused. Freedom must be guarded with structure. Territory must be defended with discipline. Vigilance is not fear; it is the stewardship of what has been won.

CHAPTER TEN

THE DANGER ZONE

Guarding What Has Been Restored

"Wherefore let him that thinketh he standeth take heed lest he fall."
1 Corinthians 10:12

There is a season after breakthrough that requires more discipline than the battle itself. This is a counterintuitive truth that surprises most people who have experienced genuine deliverance. The season of battle is characterized by urgency, by prayer that is desperate, by conviction that is sharp, by the clear awareness that something must change or the cost will be unbearable. That urgency is a powerful motivator. But urgency is not a sustainable foundation. And when it fades, as it inevitably does, what replaces it determines whether freedom endures or erodes.

Victory is visible. Vigilance is quiet. After deliverance, stability begins to return. Routine settles in. Crisis fades. The intensity that once drove fervent, desperate prayer softens into something more comfortable. And this is the danger zone, not because you are weak in this season, but because you are comfortable. And comfort, without structure, is one of the most effective environments for slow spiritual erosion.

How Relapse Actually Happens

Most people imagine relapse as a single dramatic moment, a sudden, catastrophic decision that undoes months or years of freedom in an instant. Relapse is almost never a single event. It is the final, visible consequence of a process that began much earlier and progressed through several stages, each of which was an opportunity for a course correction that was not taken.

It begins with the loosening of a single discipline. Prayer becomes slightly less consistent. Scripture reading becomes occasional rather than daily. The accountability conversation that should happen is repeatedly postponed. None of these individual adjustments feel significant at the time. Each one has a reasonable justification, life is busy, the breakthrough was genuine, the crisis that drove the urgency has passed, and the season of maximum vulnerability feels like it is behind you. The danger of this reasoning is not that it is entirely wrong. The danger is that it uses accurate observations, the breakthrough was real, the worst season is behind you, to justify a conclusion that is spiritually dangerous: that the structure which produced the freedom is no longer necessary now that the freedom has arrived.

From the loosened discipline, the process moves to the reappearance of provision. The environment that fed the former pattern becomes accessible again, not necessarily through deliberate reintroduction, but through the gradual removal of the boundaries that had kept it at a distance. The digital habit that was guarded begins to drift. The relationship that was held at arm's length begins to edge closer. The mental space that was filled with truth begins to lose its intentionality. And slowly, the supply lines that were deliberately cut during the breakthrough season begin to reopen. The final stage before visible relapse is the return of the familiar narrative, the old voice that knew your name before you knew your freedom, that speaks in the first person and feels entirely internal, that argues with tremendous sophistication for why a return to the former pattern is reasonable, understandable, perhaps even inevitable. By the time this voice returns with full force, the disciplines are weakened, the provision has been restored, and the structure that once held everything together has been quietly dismantled. What follows is not a surprise. It is the logical outcome of a process that began long before the moment of visible collapse.

Understanding this progression is not meant to produce anxiety. It is meant to produce strategic vigilance. If you can identify the first stage, the loosening of a single discipline, as the beginning of a dangerous trajectory rather than an innocent adjustment, you can make a course correction before the process reaches its conclusion. The danger zone is not primarily the moment of temptation. It is the drift that precedes it. Guard the beginning, and you protect the end.

The Anatomy of Drift

The danger zone does not announce itself. It does not arrive with a dramatic temptation that triggers all your alarm systems. It comes gradually, through a sequence of small decisions that individually feel manageable but collectively represent a significant shift in trajectory. It is like a riptide in the ocean. A riptide doesn't announce itself with crashing waves or violent motion. It looks calm and inviting on the surface.

This is what drift looks like in practice: prayer moves from daily to occasional to irregular to rare. Disciplines that were essential during the battle are quietly renegotiated as the urgency fades. Boundaries that were firm during crisis soften as stability makes them feel unnecessarily restrictive. Accountability that was sought during the worst moments is released as independence is reclaimed.

Each of these adjustments can feel entirely reasonable. And individually, perhaps none of them is catastrophic. But cumulatively, they represent the reopening of access points that were deliberately closed. They represent the slow return of provision for patterns that were evicted. And by the time the consequences become visible, the drift has been happening for a long time.

"Be sober, be vigilant; because your adversary the devil, as a roaring lion, walketh about, seeking whom he may devour." **1 Peter 5:8**

Sobriety implies clarity, the willingness to see your situation accurately rather than through the optimistic haze of post-deliverance confidence. Vigilance implies watchfulness, the ongoing, active awareness of vulnerability rather than the assumption of permanent security. The enemy rarely attacks where you are most guarded. He is patient. He observes where vigilance fades, where disciplines have loosened, where comfort has replaced alertness. And then he moves.

The House That Was Swept and Empty

Jesus provided one of the most sobering pictures of post-deliverance vulnerability in the Gospel of Luke. When an unclean spirit is cast out, He said, it goes through dry places seeking rest. Finding none, it returns to its former habitation. And if it finds that house swept and garnished, cleaned up, made presentable, but empty, it goes and brings seven other spirits more wicked than itself, and the last state of that person is worse than the first. The critical phrase is "swept and garnished." The house was clean. The visible evidence of former occupation had been removed. But it was empty. Cleaning is not the same as filling. Eviction is not the same as habitation. Freedom is not sustainable in a vacuum. The space that deliverance creates must be intentionally filled with spiritual discipline, with aligned community, with the ongoing practice of abiding in Christ, with truth that renews the mind and structures the interior life around what is eternal and holy rather than familiar and destructive.

> *"But put ye on the Lord Jesus Christ, and make not provision for the flesh, to fulfil the lusts thereof."*
>
> **Romans 13:14**

Provision means supply. It means accessibility. If the access points that fed former patterns remain available, even in reduced form, even in a version that feels less threatening than before, they represent ongoing provision for the flesh. And provision for the flesh is preparation for relapse. Freedom must be fortified, not merely celebrated.

REFLECTION

- Have I relaxed disciplines since my breakthrough that once protected what was restored?
- Where might subtle erosion be occurring in my life right now?
- Do I still maintain provision for patterns I claim to have surrendered?
- Am I sober and vigilant, or have I become comfortable and distracted?

APPLICATION

- Reestablish one spiritual discipline that has weakened since your breakthrough.
- Remove one source of silent provision that continues to feed a former pattern.
- Reinforce accountability intentionally and specifically, not just generally.
- Evaluate your current environment honestly for subtle sources of erosion.

PRAYER

Father, guard me in seasons of stability. Keep me sober and vigilant when comfort tempts me to lower my guard. Strengthen my disciplines and remove any complacency that has quietly settled in. Teach me to fortify what You have restored rather than simply celebrate it. I refuse to drift. I choose vigilance. In Jesus' name, Amen.

DECLARATION

I remain vigilant.

I guard restored territory.

I remove provision for the flesh.

I build enduring structure.

I refuse the return narrative.

No pigs allowed.

CHAPTER ELEVEN
JEWELS FROM THE PIGPEN

Wisdom Extracted from Consequence

"And we know that all things work together for good to them that love God, to them who are the called according to his purpose."

Romans 8:28

Some lessons are learned through instruction. Others are learned through consequences. There are things you can only know from the inside of the experience, truths that no sermon can fully transfer, no book can completely convey, no well-meaning mentor can deliver to you from the outside. They must be lived. They must be felt. They must be walked through in the darkness of your own season. And then, once you have come through, you discover that what appeared to be only destruction was also formation.

The pigpen was not designed as destiny. It became a classroom. And like all classrooms, what matters most is not how long you stayed but what you carried with you when you left.

Conquer or Be Conquered (Lessons from the Wild)

A few years ago, I had the privilege of visiting a safari in South Africa. I went intending to see the king of the jungle, which happens to be the lion. A lion is often associated with being an undefeated, ferocious animal. The very thought of them somehow creates a certain level of fear and intimidation. As a result of their reputation and killer instinct characteristics, they cause even the strongest individual to retreat or become hopeless when encountering one. Although their characteristics warrant fear, a few people have been known to conquer a lion. This brings a profound level of merit and grit. However, the ability to encounter or be entangled with a lion, survive, and conquer it is one that brings great honor.

The tour guide gave us safety information and drove us through the safari to view the various animals. One of the things that left an indelible imprint on my mind was the commentary on the food chain within the safari. The bigger, more ferocious animals preyed on animals that were harmless in nature. Some of the animals had to eat or be eaten. Their survival depended on their ability to conquer that which was trying to conquer them. I reflected on the process of conquering versus being conquered. What determined which animal subdued the other in their quest to survive? A couple of observations brought me to some conclusions.

The first was the ferocity of the animal. Ferocity is often the defining trait that allows an animal to survive in a world ruled by competition and danger. In the wild, being ferocious does not always mean being reckless, but it does mean having the courage, aggression, and determination to defend territory, protect oneself, or secure sustenance. A ferocious animal is less likely to be seen as easy prey. This fierce nature becomes one of its main survival tools and establishes strength in its environment. This is an imperative characteristic, not just for an animal in the safari, but for an individual who has decided to leave the pigpen of issues that life has placed them in.

Secondly, there was the innate ability to dodge danger. Some animals possess the ability to detect danger and run the other way. This innate ability is a gift that both animals and people who desire to conquer must learn to sharpen. In the wild, survival often depends on the quickness to shift directions, avoid attacks, and use agility as a weapon against threats. An animal that can leap high to escape a predator or crouch low to stay undetected shows how flexibility and awareness are just as powerful as brute strength. Likewise, a person who desires to overcome life's obstacles must cultivate the same instincts, knowing when to rise above challenges, when to stay grounded, and how to move strategically to avoid unnecessary setbacks.

Equally important is the instinct to collaborate. Many animals succeed not by going at it alone, but by working in groups, uniting their efforts to take down prey much larger or stronger than themselves. Lions hunt in prides, wolves move in packs, and even smaller creatures form alliances to survive. This mirrors the path of a person who longs to be a conqueror. True greatness is not only in personal strength, but also in recognizing the value of teamwork. By aligning with others who share the same vision, multiplying efforts, and compensating for weaknesses, one can achieve victories that would be impossible alone. In the end, agility and collaboration become the twin pillars of conquest.

In life, we can borrow from some of the strategies just mentioned, not only to exit the pigpen but also to withdraw priceless things with intention and precision. One of the most powerful approaches is adopting the mindset of ferocity, the relentless drive of an individual whose goal is to defeat anything that tries to pull them under. This is not about recklessness or aggression, but rather about cultivating a focused determination that refuses to surrender to circumstances, setbacks, or the pressures that attempt to destabilize us. Just like a seasoned warrior, this kind of ferocity is disciplined, strategic, and unwavering in the pursuit of victory.

Ferocity says that you not only pursue deliverance, but that you refuse to stop until you have tangible evidence of victory in your hands. It means you move with intentional focus, unshakable determination, and a fire that will not be quenched by resistance or by the things that once tried to conquer you. Ferocity testifies that you do not just go after something, you conquer it, you master it, and you return with undeniable proof that it was worth the fight.

A person who embodies this ferocious characteristic understands that obstacles are not roadblocks but opportunities to sharpen their resolve. Every challenge that appears to be insurmountable becomes a testing ground for resilience, courage, and creativity. They approach life with a mindset that no situation is too difficult to overcome if it is faced with clarity, preparation, and relentless persistence. By studying and emulating this kind of determination, we can learn to confront our own struggles head-on rather than allowing them to dictate our path.

Ferocity also involves a deep awareness of one's own strengths and limitations. It is about understanding the terrain of your life, the areas where you can assert control, and the areas that require patience and adaptation. This kind of strategic intensity ensures that energy is not wasted on battles that are unnecessary or misaligned with our ultimate goals. By channeling our focus where it matters most, we preserve our stamina, sharpen our effectiveness, and maintain the momentum needed to triumph over challenges

Sometimes you must go through the mud to recognize your worth and to appreciate the power of restoration. Those jewels remind you that you survived what was meant to destroy you, and now you carry the brilliance of someone who has been tried by fire but came out purified.

Carrying the Jewels Without Carrying the Shame

There is a critical distinction that must be made when it comes to the wisdom extracted from difficult seasons: the difference between carrying the lesson and carrying the shame. Both are possible. And for many people who have experienced genuine deliverance and walked through the process of confronting the "pigs" in their lives, the temptation is to carry both and to take the insight forward while continuing to drag the shame as though it were a penance that still needed to be paid.

Shame is not a jewel. It is weight. It has nothing to teach you that has not already been taught by the consequence itself. If consequence produced clarity, shame adds nothing to that clarity except the prolonged suffering of a sentence that has already been served. The prodigal son's father did not place a scarlet letter on his son's robe when he returned. He placed the best robe over him. He did not build a monument to the pigpen season as a reminder of what the son had wasted. He threw a party. Restoration in God's economy is not accompanied by the ongoing rehearsal of what made restoration necessary. It is marked by the total and lavish replacement of what was lost.

This does not mean you forget. You cannot and should not forget. The memory of what the pigpen cost you is part of what makes the jewels so valuable. A person who has forgotten their consequence cannot steward their freedom with the same intentionality as one who remembers clearly what was at stake. But there is a profound difference between a memory that informs your stewardship and a memory that defines your identity. The first is wisdom. The second is bondage in a different form.

Carrying the jewels forward means allowing what the season taught you to make you humbler, more discerning, more compassionate toward others in similar seasons, and more structurally intentional about the life you are building. It means turning the curriculum of your consequence into the architecture of your freedom. What the pigpen exposed about the danger of independence, you carry as a commitment to covering. What it revealed about the inadequacy of inheritance without maturity, you carry as a commitment to formation before function. What it taught you about the cost of drift, you carry as a commitment to vigilance. The jewels are not trophies to display. They are tools to deploy in the construction of a life that does not have to repeat what it has already learned.

The Prodigal's Journey

Luke 15 records the familiar account of the prodigal son, a story so well-known that we can sometimes read past its depth without pausing to sit in what it is saying. The son's descent did not begin with "pigs". It began with a demand for inheritance before maturity had been established. He wanted what belonging would eventually have produced, but he wanted it now, on his own terms, without the formation that would have made him ready to steward it.

> *"Father, give me the portion of goods that falleth to me."* **Luke 15:12**

Inheritance without maturity is dangerous. Independence without formation invites famine. This is not simply a story about a young man who made poor financial decisions. It is a story about the theological reality that covering, formation, and alignment under godly authority exist not to restrict us but to protect us from the consequences of receiving gifts we are not yet equipped to carry.

The far country represents the place of unsupervised independence, the space where there is no one to challenge your direction, no covering to protect your process, and no voice close enough to interrupt your drift before it becomes catastrophe. Distance always precedes depletion. The further he moved from the father's house, the more vulnerable he became to the exact kind of famine he had never anticipated.

What the Pigpen Teaches

The pigpen is the lowest point in the story, the place of maximum consequence and minimum dignity. It is the place where everything the son had attempted to build on his own has collapsed, where the illusions he traveled to the far country to pursue have been fully exposed as empty, and where the only thing left is the raw reality of what independence without alignment produces.

But notice what happened there.

> *"And when he came to himself..."* **Luke 15:17**

Clarity returns in consequence. In the pigpen, stripped of everything that had obscured his judgment, the son came to himself, recovered his actual perception of reality, remembered what home was, and understood for the first time what his departure had cost him. This is the jewel hidden in the pigpen: the clarity that comfort obscures and consequence reveals. What could not be taught through instruction was learned through loss. What could not be communicated through relationship was communicated through need. The pigpen teaches several specific truths that are worth extracting and carrying forward. First, unmanaged independence produces vulnerability, covering rejected becomes protection forfeited. Second, inheritance without discipline collapses quickly, because blessing requires the formation to sustain it. Third, distance distorts perception, in proximity to the father, provision was normal; in the far country, survival became a struggle. Fourth, consequence clarifies priorities; comfort may hide truth, but hardship reliably exposes it.

Restoration Is Not Partial

The son's return is one of the most theologically rich moments in all of Jesus' teaching. He rose and went to his father. He rehearsed his confession on the way. He planned to ask only for servant status, having lost, in his own assessment, any right to sonship. But the father saw him while he was still a great way off and ran. Not walked. Ran.

> *"But when he was yet a great way off, his father saw him, and had compassion, and ran, and fell on his neck, and kissed him."* **Luke 15:20**

The robe covered what consequence had stripped bare. The ring restored the authority that independence had squandered. The shoes confirmed a sonship that the son believed he had forfeited beyond recovery. And the feast declared that what was lost, truly and genuinely lost, had been found. Restoration in God's economy is not partial. It is not proportional to the severity of what was lost. It is comprehensive, lavish, and rooted in a love that runs toward us before we have finished formulating our apology. But wisdom must be extracted, or consequence will be wasted. If the pigpen only produces shame, growth stalls. If it produces insight, honest, specific, actionable insight, then maturity develops. You are not called to relive former bondage. You are called to learn from it so thoroughly that what you carry out of the pigpen becomes the very foundation of the stability you build going forward.

REFLECTION

- What did my lowest season teach me that I could not have learned any other way?
- Did I extract wisdom from my consequence, or have I only carried shame?
- What patterns did my pigpen season expose that I need to address structurally?
- Have I truly received restoration, or am I still rehearsing shame instead of living in freedom?

APPLICATION

- Write down three specific lessons learned from a season of difficulty or consequence.
- Identify one discipline in your current life that was built directly from past consequence.
- Release shame specifically through confession and replace it with deliberate gratitude.
- Commit to living differently based on what insight has revealed; not just emotionally, but structurally.

PRAYER

Father, thank You for mercy in seasons of consequence. Help me extract wisdom from every failure and humility from every correction. Let the lessons I have learned become the stability I now walk in. Restore what was lost and strengthen what was weak. I choose maturity over regret, and I choose to carry what the pigpen taught me as a jewel, not a scar. In Jesus' name, Amen.

DECLARATION

I extract wisdom from consequence.

I receive restoration fully.

I walk in humility.

I live with disciplined insight.

I refuse the return narrative.

No pigs allowed.

SECTION VI
GOVERNANCE

Living as a Champion and Sustaining Victory

— — —

Deliverance restores possibility. Governance sustains it. You were not freed merely to survive, and you were not delivered simply so that the "pigs" would be gone. You were freed to govern. There is a vast and important difference between being delivered and being established, between the moment of release and the lifetime of ordered freedom that follows it.

Deliverance breaks chains. Governance prevents them from being reattached. Deliverance removes what was holding you back. Governance ensures that what was removed stays removed, not through fear or white-knuckled resistance, but through the structured, intentional, Spirit-sustained authority of a life that has been genuinely transformed. This final section moves beyond reaction into architecture. Beyond avoidance into authority. Champion identity is not motivational language. It is theological reality rooted in union with Christ. And governance must endure.

CHAPTER TWELVE

THE CHAMPION

Formed for Dominion

"Let us make man in our image, after our likeness:

and let them have dominion..."

Genesis 1:26

Deliverance restores possibility. Governance sustains it. You were not freed merely to avoid failure. You were formed to exercise dominion, and that is a theological statement before it is a motivational one. Genesis 1:26 does not present dominion as a reward for exceptional spiritual performance. It presents it as part of the original design. Dominion was woven into humanity at creation. It was not lost at the Fall in the sense of being permanently revoked. It was compromised, distorted, and subjected to the bondage of sin. But redemption, at its core, is the restoration of what the Fall interrupted, including the capacity for genuine, Spirit-governed dominion.

A champion, in the framework of this book, is not defined by the absence of difficulty. A champion is defined by formed character, the steady, tested, obedient character that has been shaped through exposure, excavation, the confrontation of internal saboteurs, the breaking of soul ties, the pursuit of wholeness, the practice of vigilance, and the extraction of wisdom from consequence. Everything that came before this chapter was formation. This chapter is the description of what that formation produces. One of my favorite forms of entertainment growing up was to watch wrestling or what is known as WWE on Monday nights. Wrestling is a physical competition between two (occasionally more) competitors who attempt to gain and maintain a superior position. It is a combat sport involving techniques such as clinch fighting, throws and takedowns, joint locks, and pins. The sport, though theatrical for entertainment, is also a good source of strategy and genuine competitiveness. Understanding the true dynamics of defeating your "pigs", also entails taking a didactic approach by looking at the actual sport of wrestling. Although it is natural and external, and even entertaining. There is a direct correlation between the sport of wrestling and winning over negative strongholds. I enjoyed the humor, the drama and what appeared to be two opponents throwing each other around in the wrestling ring. I particularly enjoyed watching the undefeated champions from the 80s to 90s, like MR. T, Hulk Hogan, Booker T. Washington, and Stone-Cold Steve Austin. These men were great entertainers who possessed a certain level of skill to not just leave the audience dazzled but also end the night as the winners. Gaining the gold belt was a big deal.

My favorite of all time wrestlers to watch was a huge framed French athlete named Andre the Giant. He was also known as the "eighth wonder of the world" This man stood erect over 7 feet tall and weighed close to 520 pounds. Andre the Giant was almost unstoppable and undefeated. His presence and statue alone brought a sense of intimidation. He was legendary, and a wonder to see. When he stepped into the ring, he commanded the audience's attention. His wins were almost effortless, and his confidence was nothing short of remarkable. I learned so much watching him and can look back today at some of his best techniques. One of his signature moves was to get his opponent down to the floor of the ring and then jump on top of them. He would put all his weight on them. He was abnormal in stature but used what many laughed at as an advantage to win. He was my wrestling hero because he was hard to conquer. The first time this giant lost a wrestling match left me in tears like a kid. His competitor was a wrestler who was relatively new on the scene. His name was Hulk Hogan. Hogan was shorter and smaller than Andre the Giant. He was probably a little over 6 feet tall.

Yet he was one of the first wrestlers brave enough and strong enough to beat this giant in the ring. I can vaguely remember watching that night when the one who had never been defeated was conquered by The Hulk. It was an unforgettable sight. Thousands of people watched as Hulk Hogan picked up this 7-feet-5-inches, 520-pound man and body slammed him. It was said that Hulk attempted to body slam his opponent earlier in the wrestling match and failed. But mustered up some strength and "hulked up" closer to the end of the match at WrestleMania and did what he attempted to do earlier.

'Andre the Giant' was an immovable force who seemed almost unbreakable, but he was met by an irresistible force. When Hogan was asked how he was able to win the wrestling match. He stated that Andre the Giant would play a lot of mind games with his opponents.

He would first beat them mentally. In other words, he would cause them to see themselves defeated before they even stepped in the ring or started wrestling. Hulk Hogan knew this was his strategy and did not allow the mind games to impact him. In an interview, he stated, "This was the perfect time, perfect place, with the perfect people to win." He seized the moment and won. This is your perfect time to reach deep down and pull out the champion that is within you. You are bigger and stronger than the "pigs" that have infiltrated your life. You are smarter than the mind games that Satan and his cohorts play on you. See yourself as a pig chaser and a pig conqueror. You may not believe it, but there is a great winner inside you who is waiting to beat the odds, overcome challenges, break the habit, move past limitations, and succeed.

The Disciplines That Sustain Dominion

Dominion is not self-sustaining. It requires active, ongoing investment in the practices that keep its foundations strong. The believer who experiences a season of genuine authority and then coasts on the momentum of that season, without continuing to invest in the disciplines that produced it, will find that the dominion fades.

Not because God withdrew it, but because the conditions that supported it were gradually dismantled through neglect.

The first practice that sustains dominion is consistent self-examination. The champion does not assume that because yesterday was victorious, today is automatically secured. They examine themselves regularly and honestly, not with the destructive gaze of condemnation, but with the clear, calibrated gaze of a steward who takes their responsibility seriously. Am I drifting? Are there access points that have quietly reopened? Are my disciplines holding? Is my interior life reflecting the freedom that deliverance produced? These are not anxious questions. They are the questions of someone who understands that governance requires attention.

The second practice is the maintenance of relational accountability. The champion does not graduate beyond the need for covering. They recognize that the authority they carry is sustained in part by the alignment they maintain, under God and under the godly voices He has placed in their life. When that alignment weakens, when the accountability relationships are allowed to drift into superficiality, the protective structure that they provide is quietly lost. And the enemy, who is always observing these things, takes note.

The third practice is the continued, deliberate feeding of the spirit. The flesh does not stop requiring management because freedom has been achieved. It requires ongoing mortification, ongoing discipline, ongoing refusal to provide it with what it uses to assert its authority. Every time you choose prayer over distraction, Scripture over entertainment, worship over worry, and submission over pride, you are maintaining the spiritual metabolism that keeps dominion alive and active. Stop feeding the spirit and the flesh will reclaim the space that surrender once yielded. These are not burdens. They are the practices of someone who has learned the cost of their absence.

Formation Precedes Function

David's story, which has threaded through several chapters of this book, provides the most instructive biblical picture of the champion's journey. He was not crowned in the valley of Goliath. The valley was the public expression of a formation that had been happening in obscurity for years, in the fields, in solitude, in encounters with adversity that no one witnessed and no one recorded. Goliath revealed what private formation had produced. The throne required even more.

"For whom he did foreknow, he also did predestinate to be conformed to the image of his Son..." **Romans 8:29**

Conformity to Christ is the goal of formation, and it produces maturity, the kind of maturity that creates stability, and the kind of stability that enables genuine governance. Authority without formation produces pride. Authority after testing produces wisdom. And wisdom is what sustains victory when the urgency of the battle has faded and ordinary life returns.

The Champion Governs Internally First

One of the most important truths about champion identity is that it governs internally before it leads externally. External authority that has not been preceded by internal governance is unstable. It is the spiritual equivalent of a building with a beautiful facade and an inadequate foundation, impressive until the pressure comes.

"He that is slow to anger is better than the mighty; and he that ruleth his spirit than he that taketh a city." **Proverbs 16:32**

Self-governance, the disciplined management of thought, emotion, impulse, and response, is described here as a greater accomplishment than military conquest. If you cannot govern your emotional responses, success will destabilize you. If you cannot govern your thought life, influence will corrupt you. The champion is first and foremost a governor of their own interior world, and everything that flows outward, their relationships, their leadership, their testimony, reflects the quality of that internal governance.

Champion identity refuses the return narrative not because of fear, but because of formation. It is no longer survival language, "I am trying not to go back." It is stewardship language, "I am governing what has been restored." You guard territory because you understand its cost. You build structure because you value the inheritance you are now stewarding. And you remain submitted under authority because you understand that authority without submission is not dominion, it is pride. Being a champion is not just a momentary thing. It must become a lifetime decision to sustain a particularly positive lifestyle. You must ask yourself the question, do I just want to conquer what I am dealing with today and fall prey to it again tomorrow? Your resolution should always be to remain undefeated.

Don't just conquer the "pigs". Never allow them to regain power over your life. Manage your freedom daily. God takes the taste out of your mouth, the thought out of your mind and the desire out of your heart. But it becomes your responsibility to maintain your wins. Every day you get up, you must decide, I still choose to win.

Abiding Is the Sustaining Practice

> *"Without me ye can do nothing."* **John 15:5**

Champion identity is not self-confidence. It is an abiding dependence. The final word on how dominion is sustained in the life of a believer is not discipline, though discipline matters. It is not structure, though structure is essential. It is not vigilance, though vigilance is required. It is abiding, and it is the ongoing, daily, moment-by-moment communion with Christ that is the source of every fruit, every strength, and every sustained victory. You are not sustained by the memory of deliverance. You are sustained by ongoing communion. The memory of what God did in a previous season will not carry you through the challenges of the current one. But the presence of God, available right now, in this moment, through prayer and Scripture and worship and surrender, is more than sufficient for everything you are facing. The champion does not coast on past victories. The champion abides consistently, humbly, dependently and finds that what they need is always available there.

REFLECTION

- Am I governing my inner life intentionally, or allowing it to govern me?
- Has the stability of recent victories quietly weakened my vigilance?
- Do I remain genuinely submitted under authority, or has success created distance?
- Am I abiding daily in Christ, or relying on the momentum of past encounters?

APPLICATION

- Strengthen one internal discipline this week; one that governs thought or emotion specifically.
- Evaluate honestly whether pride has surfaced subtly in the wake of recent victories.

- Renew your commitment to daily abiding practices with concrete, non-negotiable structure.
- Guard your spiritual influence with the ongoing humility of one who knows they can do nothing without Christ.

PRAYER

Father, form me for dominion. Keep me humble in strength and vigilant in stability. Teach me to govern my spirit first and lead from that place of internal order. Let formation outlast emotion and structure outlast passion. I choose stewardship over survival, and I choose abiding dependence over self-sufficient confidence. In Jesus' name, Amen.

DECLARATION

I am formed for dominion.

I govern my spirit.

I abide in Christ.

I guard restored territory.

I keep what was gained.

No pigs allowed.

CHAPTER THIRTEEN
SUSTAINED CHANGE

Building What Endures

"Therefore whosoever heareth these sayings of mine,
and doeth them, I will liken him unto a wise man,
which built his house upon a rock."

Matthew 7:24

Temporary change is often emotional. Sustained change is structural. This distinction carries enormous practical weight because it determines whether what God has built in you through this journey becomes a legacy or merely a season. Moments of genuine encounter with God can alter the trajectory of a life. Decisions made in the heat of conviction can spark real transformation. But endurance, the kind of endurance that produces legacy, that builds something worth inheriting, is determined not by the intensity of the beginning but by the quality of the foundation on which everything rests.

Jesus does not say the storm will not come for the wise builder. He says the house will not fall when it does. Storms are not eliminated by obedience. They are endured through foundation. And the difference between collapse and endurance, in every case, is construction. What have you been building? Not what have you been feeling, not what breakthrough have you experienced, not what declaration have you made, but what have you been constructing in the ordinary, unspectacular, unwitnessed days when no one is watching and the crisis that drove you to God has long since passed?

The Gap Between Deliverance and Establishment

There is a season that most people do not talk about enough, the gap between the moment of deliverance and the moment of genuine establishment. Deliverance is a beginning, not a destination. It is the clearing of the ground, the removal of what did not belong. But cleared ground is not yet built ground. There is a period of construction that must follow the clearing, and this period is often the most vulnerable, the most easily misunderstood, and the most consequential of the entire journey.

In this gap, the person who has been delivered often feels unstable in ways they did not expect. The urgency that drove them through the battle has faded. The community that rallied around them during the crisis has returned to its own life. The dramatic spiritual encounters that marked the deliverance season have given way to the ordinary texture of daily life. And the person stands in the cleared space, genuinely free, and realizes with some alarm that they do not yet know how to inhabit that freedom fully. They know how to fight for it. They know how to weep for it. They know how to pray for it. But they do not yet know how to simply live in it.

This is not a failure. It is a phase. And like every phase, it is navigated best by those who understand what it is and what it requires. What the gap requires is not more intensity, there has been enough of that. What it requires is architecture. The slow, deliberate, unglamorous work of building the structure that will hold what God has restored. Prayer rhythms. Accountability relationships. Environmental boundaries. Identity declarations rehearsed until they become conviction rather than aspiration. Disciplines established not in response to crisis but in anticipation of the ordinary days that are coming, the long stretch of normal life in which freedom must be lived rather than merely claimed.

The gap is also where you discover the difference between what you believed about yourself during the battle and what you believe in the quiet. During the battle, conviction runs high. The stakes are visible, the urgency is real, and the motivation to choose rightly is supported by the weight of everything that is obviously at risk. But in the quiet season, when the stakes are not visible, when no crisis is pressing, when nothing immediately terrible will happen if you lower your guard for a day, what you believe about your identity, your freedom, and your responsibility becomes clear. Sustained change begins in the gap. And it is built, brick by brick, through the repeated choosing of obedience when nothing dramatic is at stake.

Settled Identity Is the Beginning of Sustained Change

Sustained change begins with settled identity. There will be days when you do not feel free, when the memory of former bondage feels more real than the reality of current liberation. Settled identity means you have decided about who you are that is not subject to revision by your feelings, your circumstances, or the return of familiar temptation.

> *"Knowing this, that our old man is crucified with him, that the body of sin might be destroyed, that henceforth we should not serve sin."* **Romans 6:6**

Crucified identity cannot be casually resurrected. The moment you begin to identify with what Christ has crucified, to say "this is just who I am," "this is my struggle," "this is what I always come back to," you are attempting to breathe life back into something that the cross declared dead. Sustained change requires that you reckon with what Scripture has settled. The old man is crucified. The new creation stands. Your identity is anchored in what Christ has done, not in what your history has been.

The Four Pillars of Sustained Change

Sustained victory is maintained through four essential structural pillars that must be deliberately and consistently reinforced.

The first pillar is the mortification of the flesh, the ongoing, intentional removal of provision and the deliberate weakening of patterns that once ruled. This is not a one-time act. It is a lifestyle of saying no to what once said yes to you, of maintaining boundaries that keep former access points sealed, of refusing to entertain in private what you would not defend in public.

The second pillar is the renewal of the mind, the replacement of former narratives with scriptural truth, engaged consistently enough to reshape the default patterns of thought. The mind does not renew itself. It is renewed through deliberate, sustained exposure to what is true, what is honorable, what is right, what is pure, what Paul describes in Philippians 4:8 as the proper diet of a mind that is being transformed.

> *"And be not conformed to this world: but be ye transformed by the renewing of your mind..."*
> **Romans 12:2**

The third pillar is submission under authority, remaining governable, accountable, and transparent before people who have permission to challenge your direction. The champion does not graduate beyond correction. The champion chooses it, seeks it, and receives it as protection rather than threat. When you remove yourself from accountability, you remove one of the most essential structural supports of sustained freedom.

The fourth pillar is abiding in Christ, the daily, consistent, habitual practice of communion with God through prayer, Scripture, and worship. Abiding is not an activity that you add to a full life. It is the source from which a full life flows. John 15:4 makes the relationship clear: abide in Christ, and fruit is the result. Move away from that abiding, and the fruitfulness begins to fade, slowly at first, then increasingly, until what remains is the form of a free life without the substance.

Legacy Is Built Through Repetition

Here is the truth about legacy that most people underestimate: it is not built through dramatic moments. It is built through the repetition of ordinary obedience. What you do consistently, over time, in the unseen places of your life, that is what creates inheritance. That is what your children observe and absorb. That is what your community inherits from the example of your life. That is what endures after everything that was temporary has faded.

> *"His seed shall be mighty upon earth: the generation of the upright shall be blessed."* **Psalm 112:2**

Stability blesses generations. The freedom you are sustaining right now is not only for you. It is for the people who come after you, for the next generation that will not have to begin where you began because you chose to do the hard work of building what endures. You are not merely avoiding relapse. You are constructing inheritance. Every day of sustained obedience, every boundary honored, every provision removed, every discipline maintained, it is all building material. And what you build on the foundation of Christ will stand.

The return narrative must be permanently rejected. Not emotionally, not temporarily, permanently. You have seen consequences. You have extracted wisdom. You have built structure. You have embraced identity. Now endurance must protect what formation produced. You are not sustained by memory. You are sustained by communion. Governance now replaces survival. Formation now replaces fragility. And endurance secures what exposure began.

REFLECTION

- Is my foundation strong enough to endure the storms that will inevitably come?
- Have I fully embraced the settled identity of who I am in Christ?

- Am I renewing my mind consistently, or allowing former narratives to reassert themselves?
- What legacy is my current pattern of daily obedience creating for those who come after me?

APPLICATION

- Strengthen one of the four structural pillars of sustained change this month.
- Commit to daily abiding without interruption for the next thirty days.
- Remove any remaining provision for the flesh, specifically and decisively.
- Evaluate honestly whether your life currently reflects the fruitfulness of genuine freedom.

PRAYER

Father, anchor me in sustained change. Strengthen my foundation and deepen my obedience. Guard me from drift and protect me from the pride that comes when things are going well. Let sanctification continue steadily in my life; not as a burden but as the beautiful, ongoing work of a God who is faithful to complete what He begins. I choose endurance. I choose holiness. I choose abiding communion. In Jesus' name, Amen.

DECLARATION

I am established.

I am sanctified progressively.

I abide in Christ.

I build what endures.

I permanently reject the return narrative.

No pigs allowed.

CONCLUSION

Living Free, Staying Free

You have come to the end of this book. But this is not the end of the journey, it is, if anything, the beginning of the most important chapter of it. The chapters you have read were designed to move you through a specific and intentional progression: from the exposure of what did not belong, through the excavation of why it remained, past the saboteurs that operate from within, into the deeper work of untying the soul and pursuing genuine wholeness, through the vigilance required to guard what has been restored, and finally into the governance that transforms deliverance from a moment into a lifestyle.

You have confronted the "pigs". You have named them, examined them, traced their access points, and refused to go on coexisting with what was never invited. That is not a small thing. For many people, this kind of honest self-examination is the most spiritually courageous act of their lives, not because it requires dramatic action, but because it requires the kind of internal honesty that our defenses work very hard to prevent.

But freedom without vigilance is fragile. And the enemy knows this. He is not finished simply because you are. He is patient, strategic, and entirely aware of the difference between a house that has been swept and a house that has been fortified. The "pigs" that were evicted will simply not forget where you live. They will test the doors. They will look for the garage to be opened again. They will send the voice of the return narrative at the moments when your guard is lowest, and your disciplines have been loosened by comfort.

There is a word for the person who has walked through everything this book describes and is now standing in the open space of genuine freedom: steward. Not just survivor. Not just overcomer, though you are both of those things. Steward, one who has been entrusted with something of extraordinary value and who takes seriously the responsibility of managing it wisely. The freedom you now carry is not only yours. It belongs to your children, who will inherit the patterns you establish. It belongs to the people God places in your path who are still in the middle of the journey you have already walked. It belongs to the community that will be shaped by the testimony of a genuinely transformed life. You are not the end of this story. You are the beginning of what God intends to do through someone who refused to settle for "pigs".

And in those moments which will come, everything this book has built in you will matter. The exposure that taught you to name what does not belong. The excavation that taught you to address root causes rather than surface symptoms. The recognition of the saboteurs that helped you identify pride and casual permission before they became catastrophic. The breaking of soul ties that began to restore the architecture of your interior life. The pursuit of wholeness that moved you toward integration rather than compartmentalization. The vigilance that trained you to guard in seasons of stability. And the governance that is slowly making authority your language instead of survival.

You are free. Stay free. Protect it not as something fragile but as something worth the investment of your most careful stewardship. Fill the spaces that deliverance created with what is holy, life-giving, and covenant aligned. Build the structure that will hold what God has restored. Remain under covering. Stay in accountability. Keep renewing your mind. Keep abiding. And when the return narrative whispers, as it will, answer with the full weight of what you now know: I have seen where that road leads. I have extracted wisdom from that season. I have paid too high a price for this freedom to negotiate with what once held me captive.

Your freedom was never meant to end with you. It is a light for someone who is still in the dark place you have already walked through. Your testimony is not just your story; it is someone else's map. Live it with the full authority of a person who has been genuinely transformed and watch what God does with the life of someone who refused to settle for "pigs".

No pigs allowed.

GLOSSARY

Abiding

The ongoing, habitual practice of communion with Christ through prayer, Scripture, and surrender. Described in John 15 as the source from which fruitfulness flows. Abiding is not a spiritual activity added to a full schedule; it is the source from which sustainable spiritual life is drawn.

Accountability

The practice of honest responsibility before a trusted person for one's actions, decisions, and patterns. Not institutional compliance but relational transparency. Accountability functions as structural protection against the drift that isolation enables.

Champion Identity

A theological reality rooted in union with Christ, not a motivational posture. Champion identity is the recognition that dominion, governance over one's thoughts, emotions, habits, and environment, is the purpose toward which deliverance leads. It is formed through testing and sustained through humility.

Cognitive Dissonance

The psychological discomfort produced by holding contradictory beliefs or behaviors simultaneously. In spiritual terms, it is the tension between what you know to be true and what you continue to do, a tension that, when honestly examined, can become a powerful motivation toward alignment.

Covering

Protection through relational alignment under godly authority. Not control but care. Covering provides the environment of honest accountability and transparent growth that isolation cannot. The absence of covering is consistently associated in Scripture with increased vulnerability to deception and drift.

Danger Zone

The post-deliverance season in which comfort replaces urgency, discipline loosens, and vulnerability increases precisely because stability feels secure. The danger zone is not characterized by dramatic temptation but by the gradual erosion of the structure that sustained freedom.

Dominion

The original divine mandate given to humanity in Genesis 1:26, restored through redemption. Dominion is governance of one's interior life; one's territory, one's sphere of responsibility. It is the purpose toward which formation leads, and the description of what champion identity produces.

Governance

The intentional, structured management of one's spiritual, emotional, relational, and environmental life after deliverance. Governance is what transforms freedom from a moment into a lifestyle, from an event into an inheritance.

Mortification

The intentional, ongoing weakening of flesh patterns through the removal of provision, the discipline of thought, and the power of the Holy Spirit. Not suppression but systematic starvation, refusing to feed what you are seeking to eliminate.

P.I.G.S.

An acronym representing the four primary components of spiritual oppression addressed in this book: Pain, Iniquity, Guilt, and Strongholds. Each represents a distinct dimension of bondage that must be confronted, named, and addressed for sustained freedom to be achieved.

Return Narrative

The internal voice that argues for a return to former bondage, through the language of familiarity, identity, inevitability, or minimization. The return narrative must be permanently rejected through settled identity in Christ, not merely managed through emotional resistance.

Soul Tie

A deep spiritual and emotional bond formed through significant intimacy, shared experience, or trauma that continues to influence thought, emotion, and decision even after the relationship or experience has ended. Soul ties can be healthy or ungodly, depending on their origin and alignment.

Spirit of Absalom

A spiritual pattern characterized by unresolved offense, wounded pride, and strategic disloyalty toward rightful authority. Named after King David's son, whose life embodied the trajectory of unhealed bitterness becoming weaponized ambition.

Stronghold

An entrenched pattern of thought, belief, or behavior that has been reinforced over time to the point that it actively resists freedom. Strongholds are not merely habits, they are fortified positions within the interior life that require targeted, sustained confrontation.

BIBLIOGRAPHY

The Holy Bible, King James Version. (1769). Cambridge: Cambridge University Press.

Anderson, Neil T. (1990). The Bondage Breaker. Eugene, OR: Harvest House Publishers.

Bevere, John. (2004). The Bait of Satan: Living Free from the Deadly Trap of Offense. Lake Mary, FL: Charisma House.

Brown, Brené. (2010). The Gifts of Imperfection. Center City, MN: Hazelden Publishing.

Cloud, Henry, and John Townsend. (1992). Boundaries: When to Say Yes, How to Say No to Take Control of Your Life. Grand Rapids, MI: Zondervan.

Kraft, Charles H. (1992). Defeating Dark Angels. Ann Arbor, MI: Vine Books.

Meyer, Joyce. (1995). Battlefield of the Mind. New York, NY: FaithWords.

Prince, Derek. (2003). They Shall Expel Demons. Grand Rapids, MI: Chosen Books.

Seamands, David A. (1985). Healing for Damaged Emotions. Colorado Springs, CO: David C Cook.

Vine, W. E., Unger, M. F., and White, W. Jr. (1985). Vine's Complete Expository Dictionary of Old and New Testament Words. Nashville, TN: Thomas Nelson.

INDEX

A

Abiding: Chapters 9, 12, 13, Glossary

Absalom: see Spirit of Absalom

Accountability: Chapters 3, 7, 13, Glossary

Agreement (spiritual): Chapters 2, 5, 7

Authority: Chapters 1, 4, 6, 12

B

Betrayal: Chapter 6

Bitterness: Chapters 6, 8

Bondage: Preface, Chapters 1, 8

Boundaries: Chapters 7, 8

C

Champion Identity: Chapter 12, Section VI, Glossary

Cognitive Dissonance: Chapter 5, Glossary

Compartmentalization: Chapter 9

Covering: Chapter 3, Glossary

D

Danger Zone: Chapter 10, Section V, Glossary

David and Goliath: Chapter 4

Deliverance: Chapters 10, 11, 12, 13

Dominion: Chapters 1, 12, Glossary

Drift: Chapters 3, 10, 13

E

Exposure: Section I, Chapters 1, 2

Excavation: Section II, Chapters 3, 4, 5

F

Flesh, mortification of: Chapters 5, 13, Glossary

Formation: Chapters 4, 12, 13

Fragmentation: Chapter 9

Freedom: Preface, throughout

G

Garage Door metaphor: Chapter 7

Governance: Section VI, Chapters 12, 13, Glossary

Guilt: Preface

H

Humility: Chapters 6, 11, 12

I

Identity: Chapters 2, 9, 12, 13

Iniquity: Preface

Intrusion: Section I, Chapters 1, 7

Isolation: Chapters 3, 6

L

Legacy: Chapter 13

M

Mind renewal: Chapters 4, 5, 9, 13

Mortification: Chapters 5, 13, Glossary

O

Ownership: Chapter 2

P

P.I.G.S.: Preface, Glossary

Pain: Preface

Pride: Chapters 3, 6, 12

Prodigal Son: Chapter 11

Provision (removal of): Chapters 7, 10, 13

R

Repentance: Chapters 2, 6, 10

Return Narrative: Chapters 5, 10, 11, 13, Glossary

S

Sanctification: Chapters 5, 9, 13

Self-deception: Chapter 2

Soul Ties: Chapter 8, Glossary

Spirit of Absalom: Chapter 6, Glossary

Strongholds: Preface, Chapters 4, 5, Glossary

Submission: Chapters 1, 3, 6, 12

T

Territory: Chapters 1, 7, 10, 12

Trauma: Chapters 8, 9

Triggers: Chapters 3, 5, 7, 8

V

Vigilance: Section V, Chapters 10, 12

W

Wholeness: Chapter 9, Glossary

www.ingramcontent.com/pod-product-compliance
Lightning Source LLC
Chambersburg PA
CBHW021929070826
49504CB00036B/446

* 9 7 8 0 9 9 8 1 7 7 7 7 9 *